ILLUMINATING THE PATH TO THE TOEIC® L&R TEST

Michiko Ueki / Brent Cotsworth
Koichi Yamaoka / Osamu Takeuchi

KINSEIDO

Kinseido Publishing Co., Ltd.
3-21 Kanda Jimbo-cho, Chiyoda-ku,
Tokyo 101-0051, Japan

First published 2021 by Kinseido Publishing Co., Ltd.

Cover design Takayuki Minegishi
Text design   Shigoka Co., Ltd.
Illustrations   Miki Nagai

音声ファイル無料ダウンロード

https://www.kinsei-do.co.jp/download/4127

この教科書で 🎧 DL 00 の表示がある箇所の音声は、上記 URL または QR コードにて
無料でダウンロードできます。自習用音声としてご活用ください。

- ▶ PC からのダウンロードをお勧めします。スマートフォンなどでダウンロードされる場合は、
  ダウンロード前に「解凍アプリ」をインストールしてください。
- ▶ URL は、**検索ボックスではなくアドレスバー (URL 表示欄)** に入力してください。
- ▶ お使いのネットワーク環境によっては、ダウンロードできない場合があります。

◎ CD 00　左記の表示がある箇所の音声は、教室用 CD (Class Audio CD) に収録されています。

はじめに

"The real voyage of discovery consists not
in seeking new landscapes but in having new eyes."
—Proust, M

　本書は、TOEIC® L&R テストのスコアを上げることだけを目的にした教科書ではありません*。こう書いてしまうと、少し奇異な感じがするでしょう。「タイトルだって、*ILLUMINATING THE PATH TO THE TOEIC L&R TEST* じゃないか」と反論が来そうです。しかし、実際のところ、TOEIC のスコアが上がっても、本当の意味での英語力が身に付いていなければ、学んだ英語を皆さんの将来に活かせないことになり、学習の意味が薄れてしまうのです。そこで私たちは、単にテストのスコアを上げることだけを目的とせず、本書を通じて、皆さんの真の英語力を伸ばす手助けをしたいと考えたわけです。

　上記のような目的を達成するために、本書では TOEIC L&R テストへの準備の形式をとりながらも、本当の英語力向上につながる様々な工夫を取り入れてみました。例えば、

1）TOEIC L&R テスト形式に沿った大量の問題提供
2）効率的な学習・解答ストラテジーの紹介（Check Point!）
3）実際に使用されるトピック・文脈の中での問題提示
4）ノーマル、ポーズ入りの2種類の音声の提示
5）英語力向上に役立つ様々な活動の配置
6）TOEIC L&R テストの題材を活用したディクテーションの導入
7）Unit ごとに「振り返り」をする機会の設定（Review!）
8）同じ問題（文法・語彙）やストラテジーと繰り返し出会う機会の提供
9）語彙習得に特化した活動とボキャブラリー・リストの提示
10）進捗状況確認のための Review Test の導入

などがあげられます。また、皆さんに学習成果を実感していただくために、ディクテーションや Review Test、Quiz などの得点を可視化（グラフ化）するための TOEIC Progress Chart (p.13) も用意しました。

　このような特徴を持つ本書での学習を契機にして、皆さんが英語力をしっかりと身に付け、そのうえで TOEIC L&R テストのスコア向上を果たしていただければ、編著者一同、これにまさる喜びはありません。

　最後になりましたが、本書の編集にご尽力いただいた金星堂の皆さんに、心より感謝したいと思います。

*本書が対象としている学習者は、TOEIC L&R テストで500を越えるスコアをあげたいと願っている方々です。

2020年盛夏

植木美千子
Brent Cotsworth
山岡浩一
竹内　理

本書は CheckLink（チェックリンク）対応テキストです。

CheckLinkのアイコンが表示されている設問は、CheckLinkに対応しています。

CheckLinkを使用しなくても従来通りの授業ができますが、特色をご理解いただき、授業活性化のためにぜひご活用ください。

CheckLinkの特色について

　大掛かりで複雑な従来のe-learningシステムとは異なり、CheckLinkのシステムは大きな特色として次の3点が挙げられます。

1．これまで行われてきた教科書を使った授業展開に大幅な変化を加えることなく、専門的な知識なしにデジタル学習環境を導入することができる。
2．PC教室やCALL教室といった最新の機器が導入された教室に限定されることなく、普通教室を使用した授業でもデジタル学習環境を導入することができる。
3．授業中での使用に特化し、教師・学習者双方のモチベーション・集中力をアップさせ、授業自体を活性化することができる。

▶教科書を使用した授業に「デジタル学習環境」を導入できる

　本システムでは、学習者は教科書のCheckLinkのアイコンが表示されている設問にPCやスマートフォン、アプリからインターネットを通して解答します。そして教師は、授業中にリアルタイムで解答結果を把握し、正解率などに応じて有効な解説を行うことができるようになっています。教科書自体は従来と何ら変わりはありません。解答の手段としてCheckLinkを使用しない場合でも、従来通りの教科書として使用して授業を行うことも、もちろん可能です。

▶教室環境を選ばない

　従来の多機能なe-learning教材のように学習者側の画面に多くの機能を持たせることはせず、「解答する」ことに機能を特化しました。PCだけでなく、一部タブレット端末やスマートフォン、アプリからの解答も可能です。したがって、PC教室やCALL教室といった大掛かりな教室は必要としません。普通教室でもCheckLinkを用いた授業が可能です。教師はPCだけでなく、一部タブレット端末やスマートフォンからも解答結果の確認をすることができます。

▶授業を活性化するための支援システム

　本システムは予習や復習のツールとしてではなく、授業中に活用されることで真価を発揮する仕組みになっています。CheckLinkというデジタル学習環境を通じ、教師と学習者双方が授業中に解答状況などの様々な情報を共有することで、学習者はやる気を持って解答し、教師は解答状況に応じて効果的な解説を行う、という好循環を生み出します。CheckLinkは、普段の授業をより活力のあるものへと変えていきます。

　上記3つの大きな特色以外にも、掲示板などの授業中に活用できる機能を用意しています。従来通りの教科書としても使用はできますが、ぜひCheckLinkの機能をご理解いただき、普段の授業をより活性化されたものにしていくためにご活用ください。

CheckLink の使い方

CheckLink は、PC や一部のタブレット端末、スマートフォン、アプリを用いて、この教科書にある ↻CheckLink のアイコン表示のある設問に解答するシステムです。
・初めて CheckLink を使う場合、以下の要領で **「学習者登録」** と **「教科書登録」** を行います。
・一度登録を済ませれば、あとは毎回 **「ログイン画面」** から入るだけです。CheckLink を使う教科書が増えたときだけ、改めて **「教科書登録」** を行ってください。

CheckLink URL

https://checklink.kinsei-do.co.jp/student/

登録は CheckLink 学習者用 **アプリ**が便利です。ダウンロードはこちらから ▶▶▶

▶学習者登録 (PC /タブレット/スマートフォンの場合)

①上記 URL にアクセスすると、右のページが表示されます。学校名を入力し「ログイン画面へ」を選択してください。
  PC の場合は 「**PC 用はこちら**」 を選択して PC 用ページを表示します。同様に学校名を入力し「ログイン画面へ」を選択してください。
②ログイン画面が表示されたら 「**初めての方はこちら**」 を選択し「学習者登録画面」に入ります。

③自分の学籍番号、氏名、メールアドレス(学校のメールなど**PC メールを推奨**)を入力し、次に**任意のパスワード**を8桁以上20桁未満(半角英数字)で入力します。なお、学籍番号はパスワードとして使用することはできません。
④「パスワード確認」は、❸で入力したパスワードと同じものを入力します。
⑤最後に「登録」ボタンを選択して登録は完了です。次回からは、「ログイン画面」から学籍番号とパスワードを入力してログインしてください。

▶教科書登録

①ログイン後、メニュー画面から「教科書登録」を選び（PC の場合はその後「新規登録」ボタンを選択）、「教科書登録」画面を開きます。

②教科書と受講する授業を登録します。
教科書の最終ページにある、**教科書固有番号**のシールをはがし、印字された**16桁の数字とアルファベット**を入力します。

③授業を担当される先生から連絡された**11桁の授業ID**を入力します。

④最後に「登録」ボタンを選択して登録は完了です。

⑤実際に使用する際は「教科書一覧」（PC の場合は「教科書選択画面」）の該当する教科書名を選択すると、「問題解答」の画面が表示されます。

▶問題解答

①問題は教科書を見ながら解答します。この教科書の  CheckLink のアイコン表示のある設問に解答できます。

②問題が表示されたら選択肢を選びます。

③表示されている問題に解答した後、「解答」ボタンを選択すると解答が登録されます。

▶CheckLink 推奨環境

PC
推奨 OS
    Windows 7, 10 以降
    MacOS X 以降

推奨ブラウザ
    Internet Explorer 8.0 以上
    Firefox 40.0 以上
    Google Chrome 50 以上
    Safari

携帯電話・スマートフォン
    3G 以降の携帯電話（docomo, au, softbank）
    iPhone, iPad（iOS9 〜）
    Android OS スマートフォン、タブレット

・最新の推奨環境についてはウェブサイトをご確認ください。
・上記の推奨環境を満たしている場合でも、機種によってはご利用いただけない場合もあります。また、
　推奨環境は技術動向等により変更される場合があります。

▶CheckLink 開発
CheckLink は奥田裕司 福岡大学教授、正興 IT ソリューション株式会社、株式会社金星堂に
よって共同開発されました。

CheckLink は株式会社金星堂の登録商標です。

CheckLink の使い方に関するお問い合わせは…

正興ITソリューション株式会社　CheckLink 係

e-mail checklink@seiko-denki.co.jp

Contents

TOEIC® L&Rテストについて

◆TOEIC（トーイック）とは、Test of English for International Communication の略称で、「英語によるコミュニケーション能力」を総合的に評価するテストです†。

◆実際の TOEIC L&R テストでは、リスニング100問（約45分）、リーディング100問（75分）の計200問を約2時間で解きます（休憩はありません）。

◆マークシート方式で、問題はすべて英語で構成されています。

◆出題内容は、日常的な話題からビジネスのシチュエーションまで多岐にわたりますが、特殊なビジネスの知識を必要とする問題は出題されません。

◆スコアは10〜990まで5ポイント刻みで算出されます。

問題形式について

リスニングセクション（約45分間：100問）*

Part 1 写真描写問題：6問
- ▶1枚の写真について4つの短い英文を聞いて、最も的確に描写しているものを選びます。
- ▶英文は印刷されていません。

Part 2 応答問題：25問
- ▶1つの質問（または発言）と3つの応答を聞いて、最も適切な応答を選びます。
- ▶質問および応答は印刷されていません。

Part 3 会話問題：39問（1つの会話につき3つの設問×13セット）
- ▶2人または3人の人物による会話と設問を聞いて、選択肢から最も適切な答えを選びます。
- ▶会話中の表現の意図を問う問題が出題されます（意図問題）。
- ▶注文書、グラフ、地図など図表を見て答える問題が出題されます（図表問題）。
- ▶会話は印刷されていません（設問および選択肢は印刷されています）。

Part 4 説明文問題：30問（1つの説明文につき3つの設問×10セット）
- ▶アナウンスやナレーションなどのトークと設問を聞いて、選択肢から最も適切な答えを選びます。
- ▶トーク中の表現の意図を問う問題が出題されます（意図問題）。
- ▶注文書、グラフ、地図など図表を見て答える問題が出題されます（図表問題）。
- ▶トークは印刷されていません（設問および選択肢は印刷されています）。

＊音声はアメリカ、イギリス、カナダ、オーストラリアの発音です。

リーディングセクション（75分間：100問）

Part 5

短文穴埋め問題：30問

▶短い文の中に1つ空所があります。
▶空所に入る最も適切な選択肢を選んで文を完成させます。

Part 6

長文穴埋め問題：16問

▶長文の中に4つ空所があります。
▶空所に入る最も適切な選択肢を選んで文を完成させます。
▶文書中に入る適切な語句または文を選択する問題が出題されます（文選択問題）。

Part 7

読解問題：54問（1つの文書：29問、複数の文書：25問）

▶Eメールや広告、記事などのさまざまな文書と設問を読み、選択肢から最も適切な答えを選びます。
▶1つの文書（シングルパッセージ）を読んで答えるものと、2～3つの関連する文書（ダブルパッセージ／トリプルパッセージ）を読んで答えるものの2タイプがあります。
▶チャット形式など、複数の人物によるやりとりに関する問題が出題されます。
▶文書中の表現の意図を問う問題が出題されます（意図問題）。
▶文を挿入する適切な位置を選択する問題が出題されます（文挿入問題）。
▶1つの文書では2～4問、複数の文書では5問の設問があります。

† その他のテスト

●TOEIC® Speaking & Writing Tests

スピーキングおよびライティングの能力を測定するテスト。スピーキングは約20分・計11問、ライティングは約60分・計8問でいずれもパソコンを使用して行われ、それぞれ0～200でスコアが算出されます（スピーキングのみのTOEIC® Speaking Testもあります）。

●TOEIC® Bridge Listening & Reading Tests

リスニングおよびリーディングの能力を測定する初中級者向けのテスト。リスニング（約25分・50問）、リーディング（35分・50問）の計約1時間・100問で行われ、30～100でスコアが算出されます。

●TOEIC® Bridge Speaking & Writing Tests

スピーキングおよびライティングの能力を測定する初中級者向けのテスト。スピーキングは約15分・計8問、ライティングは約37分・計9問でいずれもパソコンを使用して行われ、30～100でスコアが算出されます。

●団体特別受験制度（IP：Institutional Program）

一般受験の「公開テスト」のほかに、企業や学校向けの団体特別受験「IPテスト」があります。IPテストは過去に公開テストで出題された問題を使用します。

＊上記の情報はすべて2021年1月現在のものです。

TOEIC Progress Chart の使い方

　この Chart は皆さんの学習の進捗状況を可視化（みえる化）して、振り返りの機会を与え、学習動機を維持する手助けとなるように配置されています。学習を終え、記入を完了したら、切り取って担当教員に提出することも出来ます。

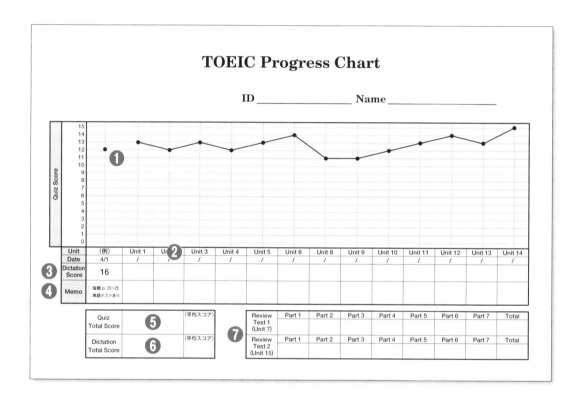

❶ Quiz Score：Quiz（小テスト）のスコアをプロット（•）してください。点を結んで折れ線グラフにすると学習状況がよくわかります。

❷ Date：授業の実施日を記入します。

❸ Dictation Score：各 Unit の Improve Your TOEIC Listening Skills! のスコアを記入します。

❹ Memo：授業の課題などがあれば、忘れないようにここに記入しておきましょう。

❺ Quiz Total Score：ここには❶の13回分の合計点を書き入れ、13で割って「（平均スコア）」の欄に自分の平均点を書き入れましょう。

❻ Dictation Total Score：ここには❸の13回分の合計点を書き入れ、13で割って「（平均スコア）」の欄に自分の平均点を書き入れましょう。

❼ Review Test 1/2：2回分の Review Test の成績を Part ごとに記入し、Total のところに合計点を書き入れましょう。

TOEIC Progress Chart

ID _____ Name _____

Quiz Score — vertical axis: 15, 14, 13, 12, 11, 10, 9, 8, 7, 6, 5, 4, 3, 2, 1, 0

Unit	(例)	Unit 1	Unit 2	Unit 3	Unit 4	Unit 5	Unit 6	Unit 8	Unit 9	Unit 10	Unit 11	Unit 12	Unit 13	Unit 14
Date	4/1	/	/	/	/	/	/	/	/	/	/	/	/	/
Dictation Score	16													
Memo	□宿題 p. 23〜25 □単語テストあり													

		Part 1	Part 2	Part 3	Part 4	Part 5	Part 6	Part 7	Total
Review Test 1 (Unit 7)									
Review Test 2 (Unit 15)		Part 1	Part 2	Part 3	Part 4	Part 5	Part 6	Part 7	Total

Quiz Total Score	(平均スコア)
Dictation Total Score	(平均スコア)

TOEIC Part **1** 写真描写問題

位 置 を 表 す 表 現 を お さ え よ う

　Part 1 では、人や物の位置に関する描写問題が多く出題されます。特に前置詞を使った表現が頻出するので、イメージと合わせて覚えておきましょう。

| on | behind | beside | above | across |

　また、位置を表す前置詞には音の脱落や連結が起きやすいので、リスニングでは気をつけましょう。　🎧 DL 002　◎ CD1-02　◎ CD1-03

　音が脱落する例：next to / at the hotel / beside the car
　音が連結する例：in a line / on it / on the top of

💎 Practice!

写真を参考にして、空所の語句を書き取ってみましょう。

🎧 DL 003 ~ 004　◎ CD1-04 ~ ◎ CD1-05

1. 　**2.**

1. Some chairs are placed ＿＿＿＿＿ ＿＿＿＿＿ ＿＿＿＿＿.

2. A man is standing ＿＿＿＿＿ ＿＿＿＿＿ ＿＿＿＿＿.

💎 Try!

下の写真に関する英文が4つ読まれます。写真を最も適切に描写している選択肢を選びましょう。

🔄 CheckLink　🎧 DL 005 ~ 006　◎ CD1-06 ~ ◎ CD1-07

1. 　**2.**

Ⓐ Ⓑ Ⓒ Ⓓ　　　　　Ⓐ Ⓑ Ⓒ Ⓓ

ＷＨで始まる疑問文を攻略しよう

WH疑問文とは、What / Where / When / Why / Who / Which / How で始まる疑問文です。これらの疑問詞がしっかりと聞き取れれば、適切な応答を容易に見つけることができます。

例えば、Where（どこで）という疑問詞の場合は、場所を指す応答が続きます。またWho（だれ）の場合は、人を指す応答が続きます。では、以下の疑問詞にはどのような答えが予想されるでしょうか。

① When [　　] ② Why [　　] ③ Which [　　] ④ How [　　]

(A) By Taxi (B) At 2:00 p.m.
(C) To report the flight delay (D) UM travel agency sounds better.

Practice!

次の各文の最初の疑問詞を書き取ってみましょう。　　　　🎧 DL 007　◎ CD1-08

1. [　　　　　　　] is going to get the bus ticket for tomorrow's tour?
2. [　　　　　　　] did you come back from your family trip?
3. [　　　　　　　] will be in charge of the new travel agency?
4. [　　　　　　　] did you call a flight attendant?
5. [　　　　　　　] travel agency would you choose?

Try!

質問文を聞き、最も適切な答えを選択肢から選びましょう。

🔄CheckLink　🎧 DL 008 ~ 012　◎ CD1-09 ~ ◎ CD1-13

1. Mark your answer on your answer sheet.　Ⓐ　Ⓑ　Ⓒ
2. Mark your answer on your answer sheet.　Ⓐ　Ⓑ　Ⓒ
3. Mark your answer on your answer sheet.　Ⓐ　Ⓑ　Ⓒ
4. Mark your answer on your answer sheet.　Ⓐ　Ⓑ　Ⓒ
5. Mark your answer on your answer sheet.　Ⓐ　Ⓑ　Ⓒ

Improve Your TOEIC Listening Skills!

Part **1** & Part **2**

TOEIC Part 1 および Part 2 形式の音声を聞き、以下の空所を埋めましょう。1回目は通常のスピードで、2回目はポーズ入りの音声が流れます。その後、1 に関しては写真を最もよく描写しているものを、2 および 3 に関しては質問文に対する最も適切な答えを選択肢から選びましょう。

※各空所はすべて正解した場合に、(　　　) は3点、(＿＿＿) は2点、(＿＿＿) は1点として採点します（部分点はありません）。

1. ⟳CheckLink 🎧 DL 013～014 ◎ CD1-14 ～ ◎ CD1-15

(A) A woman is (¹.＿＿＿＿＿ ＿＿＿＿＿
　　　＿＿＿＿＿).

(B) A woman is looking at the (².＿＿＿＿＿
　　　＿＿＿＿＿).

(C) A woman is (³.＿＿＿＿＿
　　　＿＿＿＿＿).

(D) A woman is talking with a (⁴.＿＿＿＿＿).

　　　Ⓐ　Ⓑ　Ⓒ　Ⓓ

⟳CheckLink 🎧 DL 015～016 ◎ CD1-16 ～ ◎ CD1-17

2. When are you going to (¹.＿＿＿＿＿) the (².＿＿＿＿＿＿＿＿＿) for the Mt. Fuji hiking tour?

(A) I'm sure (³.＿＿＿＿＿ ＿＿＿＿＿ ＿＿＿＿＿) there.

(B) By this Friday, (⁴.＿＿＿＿＿ ＿＿＿＿＿ ＿＿＿＿＿)

(C) It's the (⁵.＿＿＿＿＿ ＿＿＿＿＿) tour this year.

　　　Ⓐ　Ⓑ　Ⓒ

⟳CheckLink 🎧 DL 017～018 ◎ CD1-18 ～ ◎ CD1-19

3. Would you like (¹.＿＿＿＿＿＿＿＿＿＿＿), sir?

(A) Could I get (².＿＿＿＿＿ ＿＿＿＿＿), please?

(B) The pen is (³.＿＿＿＿＿ ＿＿＿＿＿ ＿＿＿＿＿).

(C) But I only need (⁴.＿＿＿＿＿).

　　　Ⓐ　Ⓑ　Ⓒ

Dictation Score	╱20

自 動 詞 と 他 動 詞 の 違 い を 理 解 し よ う

<u>自動詞</u>：後ろに目的語（名詞・代名詞）をとりません。目的語をとる場合は動詞の後ろに
　　　　前置詞が必要となります。自動詞は前置詞とセットで覚えておきましょう。

> 例
>
> account for（…を説明する）、apologize to（…に謝る）、
> arrive at（…に到着する）、complain about/of（…について不満を言う）、
> graduate from（…を卒業する）、succeed in（…において成功する）

<u>他動詞</u>：後ろに目的語（名詞・代名詞）をとります。その際、前置詞は不要です。

> 例
>
> approach（…に近づく）、attend（…に出席する）、contact（…に連絡する）、
> discuss（…を論じる）、explain（…を説明する）、marry（…と結婚する）、
> reach（…に着く）、require（…を必要とする）

◆Practice!

次の２つの文のうち、どちらが文法的に正しいかを判断し、選択肢を選びましょう。　　CheckLink

1. (A) I apologized to her for being late.
　　(B) I apologized her for being late.

2. (A) She explained the details about the flight delay.
　　(B) She explained to the details the flight delay.

3. (A) Students should attend on the orientation for the Mt. Fuji hiking tour.
　　(B) Students should attend the orientation for the Mt. Fuji hiking tour.

4. (A) The passenger complained about the in-flight Wi-Fi connection.
　　(B) The passenger complained the in-flight Wi-Fi connection.

 **Try!**

空所に入る語句として最も適切な選択肢を選び、文を完成させましょう。 CheckLink

1. Climbing Mt. Fuji ------- a lot of experience and careful preparation.
   (A) requires   (B) requires to   (C) requires about   (D) requiring

   Ⓐ Ⓑ Ⓒ Ⓓ

2. You are invited to ------- a free rafting tour down the Salt River.
   (A) joining   (B) join against   (C) join   (D) join with

   Ⓐ Ⓑ Ⓒ Ⓓ

3. Please be sure to ------- the items on the list to the hiking tour.
   (A) bring about   (B) bring   (C) bring on   (D) brought

   Ⓐ Ⓑ Ⓒ Ⓓ

4. For more detailed information, please ------- us at ABCtour@email.com.
   (A) contact with   (B) contacting   (C) contact   (D) contact through

   Ⓐ Ⓑ Ⓒ Ⓓ

5. You can ------- a reasonably priced round-the-world trip at that travel agency.
   (A) buy   (B) buy for   (C) buy in   (D) buy at

   Ⓐ Ⓑ Ⓒ Ⓓ

6. Our company has coordinators who ------- overseeing travel plans.
   (A) specialize at   (B) specialize in   (C) specialize on   (D) specialize

   Ⓐ Ⓑ Ⓒ Ⓓ

7. The travel agency ------- the featured tour next year.
   (A) discussed   (B) discussed about   (C) discussed in   (D) discussed for

   Ⓐ Ⓑ Ⓒ Ⓓ

8. Since the number of applicants for the Yellowstone National Park tour has been greatly increasing, we might need to ------- another guide.
   (A) add toward   (B) add   (C) add to   (D) add for

   Ⓐ Ⓑ Ⓒ Ⓓ

9. When you attend the one-day scuba diving course, you must ------- what the instructor says.
   (A) know   (B) talk   (C) listen   (D) obey

   Ⓐ Ⓑ Ⓒ Ⓓ

10. The pilot ------- the flight delay to the passengers.
    (A) accounted for   (B) accounted
    (C) accounted at   (D) accounted about

    Ⓐ Ⓑ Ⓒ Ⓓ

情 報 発 見 力 を 身 に つ け る の が カ ギ

Part 7 では、大量の英文を読み、問題に答えなければなりません。ここで大切になるのは、情報を見つけ出す力、つまり「情報発見力」です。この力をつけるために、設問の答えとなる根拠を常に意識するようにしましょう。

Practice!

次の文書の中で以下の設問の答えの根拠となる部分に、指定された線を引きましょう。

		指定線
1	どこで主なツアーが行われますか？	———
2	ツアーはいつまで利用できますか？	═══
3	追加料金でどのような活動に参加できますか？	------------
4	教職員1人あたりの参加費用はいくらですか？	〰〰〰

Arizona National Park Tour

March 28th — April 4th

Join ABC Outdoors as we explore several national parks located in Arizona. We'll explore the Grand Canyon, which is one of the seven natural wonders of the world. In addition to hiking and camping at the park, we will also journey to Sedona. An optional bird watching activity in Sedona is $20 extra cost. There's also water rafting on the Salt River ($40 extra).

Tour Fee

$230 — Students
$260 — Faculty staff & Alumni association members
$275 — Affiliates
$460 — Community members

Note
- If you join the bird watching activity, please bring field glasses.
- If you join water rafting, please bring your swimsuit.
- With a special coupon, you can get a **50% discount** on water rafting!

For more detailed information, please contact us at **ABCoutdoortour@email**.com. We will reply to your email within two business days.

Try!

左の文書に関する以下の設問に対して、最も適切な答えを選択肢から選びましょう。　⟲CheckLink

1. Which activities are NOT included in the standard Arizona National Park tour?

(A) The Arizona museum tour

(B) The Sedona tour

(C) Hiking at the park

(D) Camping at the park

Ⓐ　Ⓑ　Ⓒ　Ⓓ

2. Which activity does the coupon apply to?

(A) Hiking at the park

(B) Water rafting

(C) Camping at the park

(D) Bird watching

Ⓐ　Ⓑ　Ⓒ　Ⓓ

 Unit 1

□ Part 1 では、人や物の（¹.　　　　　）を問う問題がよく出題される。

□ 前置詞句を扱ったリスニングは、音の脱落〔例えば（².　　　　　）〕や、連結〔例えば（³.　　　　　）〕がよく起こるので要注意！

□ Part 2 では、（⁴.　　　　　）を聞き逃さないようにしっかり集中して聞く。

□ Part 5 では、（⁵.　　　　　）動詞と（⁶.　　　　　）動詞の違いに気をつける。目的語を後ろに必要とするのは、前者の（⁷.　　　　　）動詞である。一方、後者の（⁸.　　　　　）動詞は後ろに目的語を必要としないが、目的語をとる場合は（⁹.　　　　　）が必要となる。

□ Part 7 では、（¹⁰.　　　　　）発見力を鍛えることが大切！

Build Up Your TOEIC Vocabulary!

Traveling

単語を覚えて、30秒以内にいくつ言えるか、ペアで確認してみましょう。

手順

① 英単語を見て意味を言う役とチェックする役に分かれて、お互いの教科書を交換する。
② 英単語を見て意味を言う役は、日本語訳を筆箱などで隠す。
③ 教員の合図とともに、1〜20の英単語を見て意味を言う（わからない場合は Let me skip it! と相手に伝えましょう）。
④ チェック役は相手の答えを聞き、正解していたら日本語訳の □ ボックスに左端から✓を入れる。
⑤ 同じ手順を日本語訳→英単語でも行う。

🎧 DL 019　◉ CD1-20

1. □□□	fare	1. □□□ 運賃
2. □□□	depart	2. □□□ 出発する
3. □□□	personal belongings	3. □□□ 所持品
4. □□□	boarding pass	4. □□□ 搭乗券
5. □□□	registration	5. □□□ （宿泊）登録
6. □□□	voucher	6. □□□ クーポン券
7. □□□	regular guest	7. □□□ 常連客
8. □□□	bill	8. □□□ 請求書
9. □□□	terminal	9. □□□ 終点の、終着地
10. □□□	aisle seat	10. □□□ 通路側の席
11. □□□	book	11. □□□ 予約する
12. □□□	agency	12. □□□ 代理店
13. □□□	abroad	13. □□□ 外国で、海外で
14. □□□	transfer	14. □□□ 乗り換える
15. □□□	disposable	15. □□□ 使い捨ての
16. □□□	inquiry	16. □□□ 問い合わせ
17. □□□	transit	17. □□□ 乗り継ぎをする
18. □□□	baggage claim	18. □□□ 手荷物受取所
19. □□□	immigration	19. □□□ 入国審査
20. □□□	hotel annex	20. □□□ ホテルの別館

＊点線のところで折ると活動がしやすくなります。

TOEIC Part **1**　写真描写問題

動 作 ・ 動 き を 表 す 表 現 に 注 意 し よ う ①

　Part 1 では、人や動物の動作や、物の動きを描写している問題が好まれる傾向にあります。音声が流れる前に、どのような動作や動きを問われる可能性があるか、写真から予想してみましょう。

左の写真を見て、どのような音声が読みあげられる可能性があるか、予想問題を 2 つ作ってみましょう（日本語で解答しても構いません）。

1. _____

2. _____

Practice!

写真を参考にして、空所の語句を聞き取ってみましょう。

🎧 DL 020 ~ 021　　◎ CD1-21　~　◎ CD1-22

1. 　　　**2.**

1. The man is _____ _____ _____ .

2. The woman is _____ _____ _____ _____ at a supermarket.

Try!

下の写真に関する英文が 4 つ読まれます。写真を最も適切に描写している選択肢を選びましょう。

⟳ CheckLink　🎧 DL 022 ~ 023　　◎ CD1-23　~　◎ CD1-24

1.

Ⓐ Ⓑ Ⓒ Ⓓ

2.

Ⓐ Ⓑ Ⓒ Ⓓ

TOEIC Part **3** 会話問題

設問を先読みして聞き取りのポイントをしぼろう ①

Part 3 では、設問を先読みして聞き取りのポイントを予想してみるのもよいでしょう。例えば、設問に Why did he start the new job? とあれば、Why と new job から「新しい仕事や理由」について尋ねていることが予想されるので、その箇所に焦点をしぼって聞き取ればよいことになります。

 **Practice!**

以下の設問を先読みした場合、何に関する情報に焦点をしぼって聞き取りをするのがよいでしょうか。最も適切と思われるものを選択肢から選びましょう。　CheckLink

1. Where does the man most likely work?　　(A) 場所　(B) 形態　(C) 理由

2. What conditions are necessary for a refund?　　(A) 対象　(B) 場所　(C) 条件

3. Which item does the coupon apply to?　　(A) 対象　(B) 場所　(C) 条件

4. Who is most likely to be selected for the job?　　(A) 人物　(B) 理由　(C) 場所

 **Try!**

会話を聞き、以下の設問に対して最も適切な答えを選択肢から選びましょう。

CheckLink　　DL 024 ~ 027　　CD1-25 ~ CD1-28

1. Where does the woman most likely work?

(A) At a print shop　　　　　(B) At a book shop

(C) At a publisher　　　　　(D) At a gift shop

Ⓐ　Ⓑ　Ⓒ　Ⓓ

2. What is the man looking for?

(A) A gift for his daughter　　(B) A book for his friend

(C) Information on the artist　(D) Some tickets to a concert

Ⓐ　Ⓑ　Ⓒ　Ⓓ

3. What does the man imply when he says, "Thank you, but I'll check an online bookstore"?

(A) He thinks buying it online must be cheaper.

(B) He is buying another book.

(C) He needs it as soon as possible.

(D) He doesn't like the service.

Ⓐ　Ⓑ　Ⓒ　Ⓓ

Improve Your TOEIC Listening Skills!

TOEIC Part 3 形式の音声を聞き、以下の空所を埋めましょう。1回目は通常のスピードで、2回目はポーズ入りの音声が流れます。

※各空所はすべて正解した場合に、(＿＿＿) は3点、(＿＿＿) は2点、(＿＿＿) は1点として採点します（部分点はありません）。

DL 028 ~ 029　◎ CD1-29　~　◎ CD1-30

W: Hello. I'm calling about the school bus. It's (1.＿＿＿＿＿＿＿＿) come at 7:30, but it hasn't come (2.＿＿＿＿＿). What is going on?

M: I'm sorry, Madam. The regular bus driver (3.＿＿＿＿＿ ＿＿＿＿＿) today because he got the (4.＿＿＿＿＿), so a (5.＿＿＿＿＿) driver is driving today. Since he's (6.＿＿＿＿＿＿＿＿＿＿＿) the route, it takes a little longer than (7.＿＿＿＿＿).

W: I see. Then how long do we (8.＿＿＿＿＿ ＿＿＿＿＿ ＿＿＿＿＿)?

M: I've called the teacher in charge, and she said they're (9.＿＿＿＿＿＿＿＿＿＿＿) to your bus stop. I'm sorry for the (10.＿＿＿＿＿).

上の会話に関する以下の設問に対して、最も適切な答えを選択肢から選びましょう。　⟳ CheckLink

1. What are the speakers discussing?
(A) A bus delay
(B) A bus breakdown
(C) The driver's bad manners
(D) Road construction
Ⓐ Ⓑ Ⓒ Ⓓ

2. What is the main reason for the delay?
(A) A heavy traffic jam
(B) A traffic accident
(C) The regular driver's illness
(D) The regular driver's mistake
Ⓐ Ⓑ Ⓒ Ⓓ

3. What does the man imply when he says, "I've called the teacher in charge, and she said they're (9.＿＿) to your bus stop"?
(A) The bus is coming soon.
(B) Her kids need to take another school bus.
(C) The driver loses the way.
(D) Her kids will be late for school.
Ⓐ Ⓑ Ⓒ Ⓓ

Dictation Score	/20

呼 応 を 理 解 し よ う

呼応とは、対になっている関係のものを指します。例えば、some とくれば後ろに others と続くことが予想されるような関係のことです。なお、主語と述語の数を対応させる場合にも呼応といいます。

対比の関係

 not only A but (also) B, A as well as B, either A or B, both A and B,
not A but B

主語と述語の対応

- each, every, no one, nobody, everybody, anyone, anybody は単数扱い。
- not only A but (also) B や either A or B は B に、A as well as B は A に動詞を対応させる。
- both A and B は常に複数扱い。

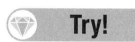

[   ] 内から正しい語句を選び、文を完成させましょう。 ⟲CheckLink

1. Both David and Brent [(A) is / (B) are] interested in jazz.

2. Either Rebecca or Matt [(A) like / (B) likes] blue.

3. Everyone [(A) like / (B) likes] potato chips.

4. [(A) Both / (B) Either] Andrew and Simon are coming to the party today.

Try!

空所に入る語句として最も適切な選択肢を選び、文を完成させましょう。 ⟲CheckLink

1. I am sure that everybody ------- the color of the dress sold on that website.
   (A) paint   (B) love   (C) loves   (D) paints

   Ⓐ Ⓑ Ⓒ Ⓓ

2. As for the T-shirts, available sizes are not only S, M, and L ------- also LL.
   (A) but   (B) or   (C) and   (D) nor

   Ⓐ Ⓑ Ⓒ Ⓓ

3. This year, I would like to grow either vegetables ------- berries in the field.
(A) but (B) nor (C) or (D) and

Ⓐ Ⓑ Ⓒ Ⓓ

4. Some people like to see movies at the theater; ------- prefer watching movies on DVD.
(A) other (B) others (C) anyone (D) everyone

Ⓐ Ⓑ Ⓒ Ⓓ

5. Surprisingly, Brenda speaks Chinese ------- Japanese.
(A) but (B) also (C) nor (D) as well as

Ⓐ Ⓑ Ⓒ Ⓓ

6. Nobody in my family, except Amy, ------- traveling by air.
(A) like (B) liking (C) are liking (D) likes

Ⓐ Ⓑ Ⓒ Ⓓ

7. You might be surprised to hear that Joseph is not a customer ------- a salesperson of the shop.
(A) but (B) and (C) or (D) as well as

Ⓐ Ⓑ Ⓒ Ⓓ

8. ------- member of the family was present at the party yesterday.
(A) All (B) Every (C) Any (D) Either

Ⓐ Ⓑ Ⓒ Ⓓ

9. Steve as well as Alan ------- to buy the outdoor gear advertised on TV.
(A) want (B) be (C) are (D) wants

Ⓐ Ⓑ Ⓒ Ⓓ

10. ------- but you knows the real price of the suit that she bought.
(A) Everything (B) Nobody (C) Anything (D) All

Ⓐ Ⓑ Ⓒ Ⓓ

タ イ ト ル か ら 文 書 の 目 的 や 内 容 を 予 測 し て み よ う

タイトルは文書の内容を簡潔にまとめたものです。これを利用して、文書の目的は何か、どのような情報が書かれているのかなどを予測してみましょう。

Practice!

以下のタイトルから予想して、最も適切と思える文書の内容を選択肢から選びましょう。

CheckLink

1. Eco-friendly Cars can Save the Earth. 　　(A) 環境　(B) デザイン　(C) 医療
2. Does Living Longer Mean Happiness? 　　(A) 交通　(B) 環境　(C) 福祉
3. Know the Market, Make a Profit. 　　(A) 投資　(B) 文化　(C) 教育
4. Two-day Clearance Sale Going on Now! 　　(A) 事件　(B) バーゲン　(C) 求人

次の文書をよく読んでみましょう。

Big Clearance Sale on Now !!

Office chairs and furniture for your home, business, restaurant, school, church or events are available from Beatle Chairs at discounted prices! In preparation for our move to a new location, all current stock must go. Shop here for the best variety and savings on seating, tables, accessories and more. Through the website, you can find even more savings, including free shipping and repairs on office chairs and a 60-day guarantee. Plus, most items in our store ship within a day. If you are one of our members, for two days only, you can get many items marked down even further on the website. Buy early for the best selection!

Try!

左の文書に関する以下の設問に対して、最も適切な答えを選択肢から選びましょう。 ⟲CheckLink

1. Why is Beatle Chairs having a sale?

   (A) It is closing one of its stores.   (B) It needs to make space.

   (C) It is relocating to another area.   (D) It is overstocked.

        Ⓐ   Ⓑ   Ⓒ   Ⓓ

2. Where can you get more of a discount?

   (A) At the retailer   (B) Through the website store

   (C) At the factory   (D) At the supermarket

        Ⓐ   Ⓑ   Ⓒ   Ⓓ

3. What service is NOT mentioned in the advertisement?

   (A) Free repairs   (B) 60-day warranties

   (C) Free shipping   (D) More discount coupons

        Ⓐ   Ⓑ   Ⓒ   Ⓓ

4. Who can get more of a discount?

   (A) Members   (B) Staff

   (C) Seniors   (D) Office managers

        Ⓐ   Ⓑ   Ⓒ   Ⓓ

Review!   Unit 2

☐ Part 1 では、(1.   ) を描写している問題が好まれる傾向にあるので、音声が流れる前に (2.   ) から予想してみるとよい。

☐ Part 3 では、設問を (3.   ) して聞き取りのポイントを (4.   ) してみるのもよい。

☐ (5.   ) とは、語句が対になっている関係のものをいう。また、(6.   ) の数を一致させる場合にも呼応という。

☐ タイトルは (7.   ) を簡潔にまとめたもの。

☐ Part 7 では、タイトルを利用して、文書の (8.   ) は何か、どのような (9.   ) が書かれているのか (10.   ) できる。

Build Up Your TOEIC Vocabulary!

Daily Life & Shopping

単語を覚えて、30秒以内にいくつ言えるか、ペアで確認してみましょう。

手順

① 英単語を見て意味を言う役とチェックする役に分かれて、お互いの教科書を交換する。
② 英単語を見て意味を言う役は、日本語訳を筆箱などで隠す。
③ 教員の合図とともに、1～20の英単語を見て意味を言う（わからない場合は Let me skip it! と相手に伝えましょう）。
④ チェック役は相手の答えを聞き、正解していたら日本語訳の □ ボックスに左端から✓を入れる。
⑤ 同じ手順を日本語訳→英単語でも行う。

🎧 DL 030　◎ CD1-31

1. □□□ price tag	1. □□□ 値札
2. □□□ discount	2. □□□ 割引
3. □□□ purchase	3. □□□ 購入する、購入
4. □□□ shopping mall	4. □□□ 商店街、ショッピングモール
5. □□□ movie theater	5. □□□ 映画館
6. □□□ art museum	6. □□□ 美術館
7. □□□ cashier	7. □□□ レジ係
8. □□□ checkout counter	8. □□□ 精算所（レジ）
9. □□□ groceries	9. □□□ 食料・雑貨類
10. □□□ convenience store	10. □□□ コンビニエンスストア
11. □□□ department store	11. □□□ デパート、百貨店
12. □□□ receipt	12. □□□ 領収書
13. □□□ bargain	13. □□□ 安売り、特価品
14. □□□ refund	14. □□□ 払い戻し
15. □□□ deliver	15. □□□ 配達する
16. □□□ fitting room	16. □□□ 試着室
17. □□□ business hours	17. □□□ 営業時間
18. □□□ carry	18. □□□ 扱っている
19. □□□ payment	19. □□□ 支払い
20. □□□ warranty	20. □□□ 保証、保証書

＊点線のところで折ると活動がしやすくなります。

TOEIC Part 1 写真描写問題

動作・動きを表す表現に注意しよう②

Part 1 では、以下のような動作・動きに関する表現がよく出題されます。聞こえた瞬間にどのような動作を指しているのか理解できるように練習しましょう。

get in the vehicle
（車に乗りこむ）

examine the menu
（メニューを調べる）

adjust a microphone
（マイクを調節する）

Practice!

写真を参考にして、空所の語句を聞き取ってみましょう。

DL 031 ~ 032　CD1-32 ~ CD1-33

1.

2.

1. A man is _____ _____ an oven.

2. A woman is _____ the customers' _____.

Try!

下の写真に関する英文が4つ読まれます。写真を最も適切に描写している選択肢を選びましょう。

CheckLink　DL 033 ~ 034　CD1-34 ~ CD1-35

1.

Ⓐ Ⓑ Ⓒ Ⓓ

2.

Ⓐ Ⓑ Ⓒ Ⓓ

TOEIC Part **4** 説明文問題

メッセージの目的を聞き取ろう

Part 4 では、1 人の読み手によるアナウンスや留守番電話のメッセージが多く出題されます。留守番電話のメッセージ形式の問題では、「なぜメッセージを残したか」「どのような変更点があるか」、そして「(話し手または聞き手の) メッセージを聞いた後の行動」を聞き取ることが大切です。

Practice!

次のメッセージを読み、その目的を選択肢から選びましょう（同じ選択肢を何回使っても構いません）。

CheckLink

1. Could you call me back? [   ]

2. The meeting will begin at 10:00, not 11:00 as was originally scheduled. [   ]

3. I'm calling you about the change to the meeting schedule. [   ]

4. If you have any questions, feel free to call me back. [   ]

(A) なぜメッセージを残したか　　(B) どのような変更点があるか
(C) メッセージを聞いた後の行動

Try!

説明文を聞き、以下の設問に対して最も適切な答えを選択肢から選びましょう。

CheckLink　　DL 035 ~ 038　　CD1-36 ~ CD1-39

1. What is the purpose of this message?
   (A) To cancel the reservation　　(B) To plan for the gourmet tour
   (C) To rearrange the reservation　　(D) To discuss the budget

Ⓐ　Ⓑ　Ⓒ　Ⓓ

2. When will the dinner begin?
   (A) At 6 o'clock　　　　　　(B) At 7 o'clock
   (C) At 8 o'clock　　　　　　(D) At 9 o'clock

Ⓐ　Ⓑ　Ⓒ　Ⓓ

3. What will the shop owner do next?
   (A) Go to the office　　　　(B) Call Judy back
   (C) Have a meeting　　　　(D) Cancel the reservation

Ⓐ　Ⓑ　Ⓒ　Ⓓ

Improve Your TOEIC Listening Skills!

Part **4**

TOEIC Part 4 形式の音声を聞き、以下の空所を埋めましょう。1回目は通常のスピードで、2回目はポーズ入りの音声が流れます。

※各空所はすべて正解した場合に、(～～～) は3点、(＿＿) は2点、(＿＿) は1点として採点します（部分点はありません）。

🎧 DL 039 ~ 040　◎ CD1-40　~　◎ CD1-41

1. Hello, Ms. Becker. This is David Anderson from West Seaside restaurant, calling to (¹.＿＿＿＿＿＿) you that your (².＿＿＿＿＿＿) is tonight at 6:00 p.m. We are keeping (³.＿＿＿＿＿ ＿＿＿＿＿) for (⁴.＿＿＿＿＿ ＿＿＿＿＿). If you have (⁵.＿＿＿＿＿ ＿＿＿＿＿) to your reservation, please (⁶.～～～～～～～～～～～～～～～) by noon.

上の伝言に関する以下の設問に対して、最も適切な答えを選択肢から選びましょう。　🔄 CheckLink

What is the purpose of the message?
(A) To remind the customer of her reservation
(B) To announce a change to the customer
(C) To discuss the budget with the customer
(D) To give a discount to the customer　　　　Ⓐ Ⓑ Ⓒ Ⓓ

🎧 DL 041 ~ 042　◎ CD1-42　~　◎ CD1-43

2. Hello, Mr. Rodriguez. This is Mark Lopez from the Moroccan Great Food Restaurant. Thank you for your (¹.＿＿＿＿＿) for the chef position. I'd like to (².～～～～～～～～～～～～～). Could you (³.＿＿＿＿＿) it to us (⁴.＿＿＿＿＿ ＿＿＿＿＿)? Thanks (⁵.＿＿＿＿＿ ＿＿＿＿＿).

上の伝言に関する以下の設問に対して、最も適切な答えを選択肢から選びましょう。　🔄 CheckLink

What is Mr. Rodriguez asked to do?
(A) Have an interview　　(B) Send a résumé
(C) Write a report　　　　(D) Meet Mr. Lopez　　Ⓐ Ⓑ Ⓒ Ⓓ

Dictation Score ╱ 20

TOEIC Part 5　短文穴埋め問題

比 較 級 や 最 上 級 を 使 い こ な そ う

　Part 5 では比較表現として、X times（twice）as＋形容詞／副詞＋as ... や as＋形容詞／副詞＋as ...、the＋比較級＋S＋V, the＋比較級＋S＋V、less＋比較級＋than ... などがよく出題されます。また、比較級や最上級を強調する副詞なども覚えておくと便利でしょう。

> 比較級を強調する副詞：far, by far, much など
> 最上級を強調する副詞：by far, ever, yet など

 **Practice!**

[　　] 内から正しい語句を選び、文を完成させましょう。　CheckLink

1. This apple is twice [(A) as / (B) so] expensive as that one over there.

2. Your portion of pasta is [(A) as / (B) so] big as mine.

3. This is [(A) by far / (B) further] the best pasta I have ever tasted.

4. The [(A) hotter / (B) hottest] the pepper becomes, the more it costs.

 **Try!**

空所に入る語句として最も適切な選択肢を選び、文を完成させましょう。　CheckLink

1. French cuisine in Japan is three times ------- expensive as that in the U.S.
(A) much　(B) more　(C) as　(D) than

Ⓐ Ⓑ Ⓒ Ⓓ

2. He is just as anxious to know about the new restaurant on Baker Street ------- you are.
(A) more than　(B) than　(C) as　(D) better

Ⓐ Ⓑ Ⓒ Ⓓ

3. The more time I spent with the chef, the more ------- I was with his culinary skills.
(A) impression　(B) impress　(C) impressed　(D) impressing

Ⓐ Ⓑ Ⓒ Ⓓ

4. Brenda says, "This is the best pizza -------."
(A) quite　(B) much　(C) as far　(D) ever

Ⓐ Ⓑ Ⓒ Ⓓ

5. The new restaurant offers ------- higher quality food than the old one.
   (A) ever   (B) much   (C) further   (D) very

   Ⓐ Ⓑ Ⓒ Ⓓ

6. A bottle of red wine is ------- expensive than white wine here.
   (A) less   (B) little   (C) no   (D) just

   Ⓐ Ⓑ Ⓒ Ⓓ

7. I like this cheese all the ------- for its bitterness.
   (A) worse   (B) worst   (C) better   (D) best

   Ⓐ Ⓑ Ⓒ Ⓓ

8. This cake tastes ------- better than that one.
   (A) much   (B) as   (C) ever   (D) further

   Ⓐ Ⓑ Ⓒ Ⓓ

9. This bakery is ------- the best in our city, offering a large variety of bread.
   (A) so   (B) by far   (C) further   (D) only

   Ⓐ Ⓑ Ⓒ Ⓓ

10. Applicants for the chef position at the restaurant should answer the
   questions on the application form as ------- as possible.
   (A) accurately   (B) accurate   (C) accuracy   (D) accuracies

   Ⓐ Ⓑ Ⓒ Ⓓ

スキャニング力を身につけよう

　スキャニングとは、特定の情報だけを探しながら読む方法のことをいいます。メニューや広告などのジャンルを読むときは、スキャニングの技法を利用すると効率的に解答にたどりつくことができます。

◈ Practice!

1. 次の文書の各カテゴリの一番安い料理に○をつけましょう。

2. 予約をする際に必要な情報はどこにありますか。該当部分に波線を引いてみましょう。

3. メインディッシュを頼みたいときはどのカテゴリを見ればよいでしょうか。□で囲んでみましょう。

Palace Hotel Restaurant

"Offering Great Dinner Specials"
3rd Ave., Monterey, CA
(006)78720382

Hors-d' oeuvre

New York Lobster Bisque $13.20
Summer Greens and Citrus Salad $10.00
Roasted Tomato and Avocado Soup .... $ 8.60

Plat de resistance

Seasoned Grilled Beef $21.90
Teriyaki Duck $20.30
Pork Chops $18.50
Grilled Seafood... $17.90

*All meals include rice or mashed potatoes, and salad.

Desserts

Spiced Chocolate Cake $11.20
Espresso Crème Brûlée $11.20
Mini Homemade Doughnuts $9.80
Vanilla Ice Cream $8.00

A 10 % discount is available until August 31.

For reservations, visit www.palacehotel.com.

Try!

左の文書に関する以下の設問に対して、最も適切な答えを選択肢から選びましょう。 CheckLink

1. Where is the restaurant located?

(A) 3rd Ave., Florida

(B) 3rd Ave., New York

(C) Monterey, California

(D) Monterey, Michigan

Ⓐ Ⓑ Ⓒ Ⓓ

2. What is included in the meals?

(A) Rice and mashed potatoes

(B) Mashed potatoes or orange juice

(C) Rice or mashed potatoes, and salad

(D) Rice or vegetables, and iced tea

Ⓐ Ⓑ Ⓒ Ⓓ

3. What will happen in September?

(A) The restaurant will be closed.

(B) The menu will be changed.

(C) The discount will expire.

(D) The voucher will be applied.

Ⓐ Ⓑ Ⓒ Ⓓ

Review Unit 3

☐ Part 1 では、(¹.   ) に関する表現がよく出題される。

☐ Part 4 では、(².   ) のような形式がよく出題される。

☐ 留守番電話のメッセージでは、「(³.   )」「(⁴.
)」、そして「(⁵.   )」を聞き取ることが大切。

☐ Part 5 の文法問題では、far、by far、much など、(⁶.   ) を強調する
(⁷.   ) や、by far、ever、yet など (⁸.   ) を強調する副詞に要
注意。

☐ Part 7 の読解問題で (⁹.   ) などを読むときは、(¹⁰.
) の技法を利用すると効率的。

Build Up Your TOEIC Vocabulary!

At Restaurants

単語を覚えて、30秒以内にいくつ言えるか、ペアで確認してみましょう。

手順

① 英単語を見て意味を言う役とチェックする役に分かれて、お互いの教科書を交換する。
② 英単語を見て意味を言う役は、日本語訳を筆箱などで隠す。
③ 教員の合図とともに、1〜20の英単語を見て意味を言う（わからない場合は Let me skip it! と相手に伝えましょう）。
④ チェック役は相手の答えを聞き、正解していたら日本語訳の □ ボックスに左端から✓を入れる。
⑤ 同じ手順を日本語訳→英単語でも行う。

🎧 DL 043　◎ CD1-44

1. □□□ expensive	1. □□□	高価な
2. □□□ reasonable	2. □□□	（値段が）それほど高くない、手ごろな
3. □□□ relocate	3. □□□	移転する
4. □□□ reservation	4. □□□	予約
5. □□□ course meal	5. □□□	コース料理
6. □□□ buffet	6. □□□	ビュッフェ（セルフサービス式の食事）
7. □□□ cuisine	7. □□□	（特定の地域などの）料理
8. □□□ culinary	8. □□□	料理の
9. □□□ refreshment	9. □□□	軽食
10. □□□ grill	10. □□□	焼き網で焼く
11. □□□ fully booked	11. □□□	満席の
12. □□□ roast	12. □□□	（直火または高温で）あぶり焼く
13. □□□ specialties	13. □□□	店の得意料理
14. □□□ serve	14. □□□	給仕する
15. □□□ atmosphere	15. □□□	雰囲気
16. □□□ quantity	16. □□□	量
17. □□□ ingredient	17. □□□	（料理の）材料
18. □□□ recipe	18. □□□	調理法
19. □□□ vegan	19. □□□	完全菜食主義者
20. □□□ beverage	20. □□□	飲み物

＊点線のところで折ると活動がしやすくなります。

TOEIC Part 1 写真描写問題

LISTENING Check Point!

細部にも注意しよう

Part 1 では、細部に関する問題が出される場合もあります。大きな動作や、目立った特徴に引きずられないように注意をしましょう。

Practice!

写真を参考にして、空所の語句を聞き取ってみましょう。

🎧 DL 044 ~ 045　◎ CD1-45 ~ ◎ CD1-46

1.

2.

1. A man is _____.

2. A man is checking his tie _____.

Try!

下の写真に関する英文が 4 つ読まれます。写真を最も適切に描写している選択肢を選びましょう。

↻ CheckLink　🎧 DL 046 ~ 047　◎ CD1-47 ~ ◎ CD1-48

1.

Ⓐ Ⓑ Ⓒ Ⓓ

2.

Ⓐ Ⓑ Ⓒ Ⓓ

依 頼 の 表 現 を お さ え よ う

　Part 2 では、依頼に対する答え方がよく出題されます。いくつかのパターンがあるので、しっかりと覚えておきましょう。特に、Do (Would) you mind -ing?「…して構いませんか」の依頼表現の場合、許可するならば No (Not at all)、断るならば Yes となるので要注意です。

以下の答え方に最も適切な依頼表現を選び、線で結びましょう。

1. Not at all　　　　　　・　　　　・ Would you give me an application form?

2. OK. I'll do it right away.　・　　　　・ Could you make a copy of this document?

3. Sure. Here it is.　　　　・　　　　・ Do you mind reviewing my résumé?

Try!

質問文を聞き、最も適切な答えを選択肢から選びましょう。

CheckLink 　　DL 048 ~ 052 　　CD1-49 ~ CD1-53

1. Mark your answer on your answer sheet.　Ⓐ　Ⓑ　Ⓒ

2. Mark your answer on your answer sheet.　Ⓐ　Ⓑ　Ⓒ

3. Mark your answer on your answer sheet.　Ⓐ　Ⓑ　Ⓒ

4. Mark your answer on your answer sheet.　Ⓐ　Ⓑ　Ⓒ

5. Mark your answer on your answer sheet.　Ⓐ　Ⓑ　Ⓒ

Improve Your TOEIC Listening Skills!

Part 1 & Part 2

TOEIC Part 1 および Part 2 形式の音声を聞き、以下の空所を埋めましょう。1回目は通常のスピードで、2回目はポーズ入りの音声が流れます。その後、1に関しては写真を最もよく描写しているものを、2および3に関しては質問文に対する最も適切な答えを選択肢から選びましょう。

※各空所はすべて正解した場合に、（＿＿＿＿）は3点、（＿＿＿＿）は2点、（＿＿＿＿）は1点として採点します（部分点はありません）。

1.

CheckLink 🎧 DL 053 ~ 054 ◉ CD1-54 ~ ◉ CD1-55

(A) People are (1.＿＿＿＿＿＿) a performance.

(B) The man is (2.＿＿＿＿＿＿) something on a whiteboard.

(C) A whiteboard has been placed (3.＿＿＿＿＿ ＿＿＿＿＿ ＿＿＿＿＿).

(D) The table has been (4.＿＿＿＿＿ ＿＿＿＿＿).

Ⓐ Ⓑ Ⓒ Ⓓ

CheckLink 🎧 DL 055 ~ 056 ◉ CD1-56 ~ ◉ CD1-57

2. Am I supposed to (1.＿＿＿＿＿＿＿＿＿＿) the résumé before the interview?

(A) You can (2.＿＿＿＿＿ ＿＿＿＿＿) it after the interview.

(B) Yes. It's (3.＿＿＿＿＿ ＿＿＿＿＿ ＿＿＿＿＿).

(C) Yes. The hotel has (4.＿＿＿＿＿ ＿＿＿＿＿ ＿＿＿＿＿).

Ⓐ Ⓑ Ⓒ

CheckLink 🎧 DL 057 ~ 058 ◉ CD1-58 ~ ◉ CD1-59

3. Are the interviews (1.＿＿＿＿＿＿＿＿＿＿) Saturdays?

(A) No, not (2.＿＿＿＿＿)

(B) (3.＿＿＿＿＿ ＿＿＿＿＿) your keys.

(C) (4.＿＿＿＿＿, ＿＿＿＿＿ ＿＿＿＿＿)

Ⓐ Ⓑ Ⓒ

Dictation Score	/20

修 飾 （ 関 係 代 名 詞 ・ 分 詞 ） を 理 解 し よ う

　名詞を修飾する場合に関係代名詞や分詞を使うことがあります。関係代名詞は必ず後ろから名詞を修飾し、分詞は前から修飾する場合と後ろから修飾する場合があります。また、関係代名詞は、前にくる名詞（先行詞）の種類と役割に応じて形式が異なります。

関係代名詞

> **例**　先行詞が人・主語の役割の例：I like <u>the man</u> **who** is standing over there.
>
> 　先行詞が物・目的語の役割の例：This is <u>the dog</u> **which** I love the most.
>
> 　先行詞が人・所有の役割の例：<u>A person</u> **whose** job is to sing is called a singer.
>
> ＊関係代名詞の that は人にも物にも使えます。

分詞 （現在分詞 -ing ／過去分詞 -ed など）

> **例**　現在分詞の例：a man **running** in the park / a **running** man
>
> 　過去分詞の例：the jewel **stolen** from the store / the **stolen** jewel

 Practice!

[　　] 内から正しい語句を選び、文を完成させましょう。　　　　　　Ⓒ CheckLink

1. The company is looking for someone [(A) who / (B) which] is good at English.

2. I want to work for a company [(A) who / (B) which] has a long history.

3. The résumé [(A) sending / (B) sent] to the personnel department was very impressive.

4. This magazine is written for people [(A) seeking / (B) sought] a part-time job.

Try!

空所に入る語句として最も適切な選択肢を選び、文を完成させましょう。　　　Ⓒ CheckLink

1. The website offers useful information for job seekers ------- are interested in working in Japan.

(A) which　　(B) who　　(C) whose　　(D) whom

Ⓐ　Ⓑ　Ⓒ　Ⓓ

2. You are welcome to join a tour of our factory conveniently ------- in the bay area.

(A) locate   (B) location   (C) locating   (D) located

Ⓐ Ⓑ Ⓒ Ⓓ

3. This is exactly the kind of job ------- I have been seeking for a long time.

(A) whose   (B) who   (C) that   (D) whom

Ⓐ Ⓑ Ⓒ Ⓓ

4. The company is planning to hire someone ------- first language is English.

(A) who   (B) whose   (C) whom   (D) which

Ⓐ Ⓑ Ⓒ Ⓓ

5. This seminar provides some tips to help people ------- a position in the financial industry.

(A) seeking   (B) sought   (C) who   (D) whose

Ⓐ Ⓑ Ⓒ Ⓓ

6. The old man ------- I saw at the airport turned out to be the founder of a famous company.

(A) to whom   (B) by which   (C) whom   (D) which

Ⓐ Ⓑ Ⓒ Ⓓ

7. The number of workers ------- from abroad has been increasing in the past ten years.

(A) employ   (B) employed   (C) employing   (D) employment

Ⓐ Ⓑ Ⓒ Ⓓ

8. ------- applicants must have a bachelor's degree in accounting.

(A) By qualifying   (B) In qualified   (C) Qualifying   (D) Qualified

Ⓐ Ⓑ Ⓒ Ⓓ

9. He applied for a position at one of the ------- electrical manufacturers in Japan.

(A) leading   (B) lead   (C) which lead   (D) who lead

Ⓐ Ⓑ Ⓒ Ⓓ

10. The man ------- contacted us yesterday by email seems to be a very promising applicant.

(A) which   (B) who   (C) whose   (D) whom

Ⓐ Ⓑ Ⓒ Ⓓ

ダブルパッセージを攻略しよう

　ダブルパッセージとは、2つの文書（例えば、広告とEメールなど）が並んだものを指します。最初のパッセージに対する反応として次のパッセージが書かれているのが通例ですので、最初のパッセージをよく読んで、条件などを確認しましょう。また、3つの文書が並ぶトリプルパッセージもありますので、それぞれの文書の関連をよく確認するようにしましょう。

Practice!

1. 次のパッセージをよく読んで、この仕事に必要とされている条件すべてに下線を引いてみましょう。

Career Opportunity: Full-time photojournalist

The Herald Times is currently seeking a full-time photojournalist. The ideal candidate must have at least five years experience as a photojournalist. He or she should also have excellent photographic and technical skills with digital cameras, strong computer skills including photography-related software, and Internet research skills. We are looking for an individual who has a master's degree in photojournalism. Successful candidates must have a positive attitude to feedback for improvement, be able to work nights & weekends, and travel as needed.

Interested candidates should send a cover letter, résumé and references to David Garcia by email at Garcia@heraldtimes.net.

---

2. 次のパッセージをよく読んで、応募者の求職上のセールスポイントすべてに下線を引いてみましょう。

To:	David Garcia <Garcia@heraldtimes.net>
From:	Shun Ree
Subject:	Your advertisement

Dear Mr. Garcia,

I am writing in response to your ad for a photojournalist. I have had ten years experience at Community Reporter Corporation as a photojournalist and feel that I am suitable for the position. I am very keen to work for *The Herald Times* because of its good reputation in this field. I'm sure that I have technical expertise and some knowledge of photo editing software. Although I do not have a master's degree, I won a Press Photo Award in 2010.

Please have a look at my attached résumé. If you feel that I am the right person for the position, please contact me for an interview. I am available every day from early next week.

I look forward to hearing from you.

Sincerely,

Shun Ree

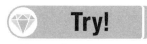

前ページの２つの文書に関する以下の設問に対して、最も適切な答えを選択肢から選びましょう。

CheckLink

1. What is this advertisement about?

(A) An advertisement for the newspaper

(B) A job advertisement for a photojournalist

(C) An advertisement for the Press Photo Award

(D) A job advertisement for a newspaper editor

Ⓐ Ⓑ Ⓒ Ⓓ

2. What is the qualification that applicants must have?

(A) Experience as a photojournalist

(B) Award experience in the field

(C) A master's degree in creative writing

(D) Computer skills including spreadsheet software

Ⓐ Ⓑ Ⓒ Ⓓ

3. What do the applicants need to send to Mr. Garcia?

(A) A cover letter and references

(B) A cover letter or references

(C) A cover letter, résumé or references

(D) A cover letter, résumé and references

Ⓐ Ⓑ Ⓒ Ⓓ

4. How should the applicant submit his/her application form?

(A) By voice mail

(B) By registered mail

(C) By telephone

(D) By email

Ⓐ Ⓑ Ⓒ Ⓓ

5. What is the condition that Mr. Ree does NOT meet?

(A) Work experience

(B) Computer skills

(C) A good reputation

(D) A master's degree

Ⓐ Ⓑ Ⓒ Ⓓ

Review! **Unit 4**

- [ ] Part 1 では、(1.) に関する問題がよく出題される。その場合、(2.) や目立った特徴に引きずられないように注意する。

- [ ] Part 2 で出題される Do (Would) you mind -ing? の応答は、許可するならば (3.)、断るならば (4.) となる。

- [ ] (5.) と (6.) は、ともに名詞を修飾する場合に利用する。関係代名詞は常に (7.) 名詞を修飾する。一方、分詞は (8.) 名詞を修飾することができ、-ing の形と、(9.) の形がある。

- [ ] Part 7 で出題される (10.) とは、2 つの文書が並んだもののことをいう。

Build Up Your TOEIC Vocabulary!

Job Hunting

単語を覚えて、30秒以内にいくつ言えるか、ペアで確認してみましょう。

手順

① 英単語を見て意味を言う役とチェックする役に分かれて、お互いの教科書を交換する。
② 英単語を見て意味を言う役は、日本語訳を筆箱などで隠す。
③ 教員の合図とともに、1〜20の英単語を見て意味を言う（わからない場合は Let me skip it! と相手に伝えましょう）。
④ チェック役は相手の答えを聞き、正解していたら日本語訳の □ ボックスに左端から✓を入れる。
⑤ 同じ手順を日本語訳→英単語でも行う。

🎧 DL 059　◎ CD1-60

1. □□□ application form	1. □□□	申込書
2. □□□ contact	2. □□□	連絡を取る
3. □□□ applicant	3. □□□	応募者
4. □□□ employ	4. □□□	雇う
5. □□□ interview	5. □□□	面接
6. □□□ personnel department	6. □□□	人事部
7. □□□ position	7. □□□	仕事の口、職
8. □□□ contract	8. □□□	契約書
9. □□□ résumé	9. □□□	履歴書
10. □□□ career	10. □□□	職歴
11. □□□ apply for…	11. □□□	…に申し込む
12. □□□ employee	12. □□□	従業員
13. □□□ academic background	13. □□□	学歴
14. □□□ employment	14. □□□	雇用
15. □□□ … industry	15. □□□	〜産業
16. □□□ skill	16. □□□	技能
17. □□□ employer	17. □□□	雇用者
18. □□□ opportunity	18. □□□	好機
19. □□□ qualification	19. □□□	資格
20. □□□ preferred	20. □□□	望ましい

＊点線のところで折ると活動がしやすくなります。

TOEIC Part 1　写真描写問題

LISTENING
Check Point!

オフィス内で使われる語句をマスターしよう

　TOEICであつかわれる単語の約7割は、ビジネスやオフィスに関連したものです。写真描写問題でも、オフィス内の様子や働いている人々が取り上げられることが多いので、オフィス内で使われる語句をイメージとともに覚えておきましょう。

左のイラストの中にある物に相当する英単語を、以下のリストから選んでみましょう。

calculator	drawer	monitor
file	document	receiver*

*電話の受話器

Practice!

写真を参考にして、空所の語句を聞き取ってみましょう。

🎧 DL 060 ~ 061　◎ CD1-61　~　◎ CD1-62

1.

2.

1. There is ＿＿＿＿＿＿＿＿＿＿＿＿＿＿＿＿＿＿ .

2. The woman is ＿＿＿＿＿＿＿＿＿＿＿＿＿＿＿＿＿＿ .

Try!

下の写真に関する英文が4つ読まれます。写真を最も適切に描写している選択肢を選びましょう。

↻ CheckLink　🎧 DL 062 ~ 063　◎ CD1-63　~　◎ CD1-64

1.

Ⓐ Ⓑ Ⓒ Ⓓ

2.

Ⓐ Ⓑ Ⓒ Ⓓ

TOEIC Part **3** 会話問題

オフィスでの頻出表現をおさえよう

オフィスでの会話のトピックには、クライアントとの予約、オフィスにある機器の故障などに関するものが多く取り上げられます。TOEICでよく出題される表現を、しっかりと覚えておきましょう。

Practice!

以下の1から6の英語表現に対応する日本語を選択肢から選びましょう。　CheckLink

1. take over someone's position [　　]　　**2.** detail(s) [　　]　　**3.** revise [　　]

4. attend [　　]　　**5.** run out of … [　　]　　**6.** behind schedule [　　]

(A) …を使い果たす	(B) 詳細	(C) 参加する
(D) 予定より遅れている	(E) …の役目を引き継ぐ	(F) 修正する

Try!

会話を聞き、以下の設問に対する答えとして最も適切な選択肢を選びましょう。

CheckLink　DL 064 ~ 067　CD1-65 ～ CD1-68

Meeting Room	Office 101	Office 102
Office 103	Office 104	Copy Room

1. What is planned tomorrow?

(A) An employee is transferred to the new department.

(B) The renovation work will be started.

(C) A new copying machine will be installed.

(D) The projector will be delivered.　Ⓐ　Ⓑ　Ⓒ　Ⓓ

2. Look at the graphic. Which office will be given to Mr. Franklin?

(A) Office 101　(B) Office 102　(C) Office 103　(D) Office 104　Ⓐ　Ⓑ　Ⓒ　Ⓓ

3. What is the man going to do in the meeting room?

(A) Make a presentation　　(B) Put the name plate on the door

(C) Check the new projector　　(D) Start the new project

Ⓐ　Ⓑ　Ⓒ　Ⓓ

Improve Your TOEIC Listening Skills!

Part **3**

TOEIC Part 3 形式の音声を聞き、以下の空所を埋めましょう。1回目は通常のスピードで、2回目はポーズ入りの音声が流れます。

※各空所はすべて正解した場合に、(_____) は3点、(_____) は2点、(_____) は1点として採点します（部分点はありません）。

🎧 DL 068 ~ 069　◎ CD1-69　~　◎ CD1-70

M: Hi, Cathy. I had to (¹·_____) the meeting early yesterday for

(²·_____) a client. (³·_____

_____) what the manager announced

at the (⁴·_____ _____)?

W: Well, our company website will be (⁵·_____) next week.

M: What will be (⁶·_____)?

W: They're (⁷·_____) a new section for employees, so you can

(⁸·_____) your company (⁹·_____ _____) from

(¹⁰·_____), as long as you have an

Internet connection.

上の会話に関する以下の設問に対して、最も適切な答えを選択肢から選びましょう。　⟳CheckLink

1. What are the speakers mainly discussing?

(A) Project deadlines　　　(B) A website update

(C) The company relocation　(D) Factory production　　　Ⓐ　Ⓑ　Ⓒ　Ⓓ

2. Why did the man leave the meeting early?

(A) To meet with his client　(B) To operate a machine

(C) To clean the office　　　(D) To prepare a document　　Ⓐ　Ⓑ　Ⓒ　Ⓓ

3. What will happen next Monday?

(A) A manager will announce the plan.

(B) A new location will open.

(C) A useful function will be introduced.

(D) A system engineer will arrive.　　　　　　　　　　　Ⓐ　Ⓑ　Ⓒ　Ⓓ

Dictation Score	/ 20

TOEIC Part 6 長文穴埋め問題

空 所 の 前 後 に ヒ ン ト が な い か 探 し て み よ う

Part 6 では、空所の前後をチェックすることによって、正解を特定できることがあります。例えば、動詞の形を問う問題であれば、空所の前後にある時や期間に関連したキーワードが正解へのヒントになるでしょう。

Practice!

次の文の時や期間に関連したキーワードに下線を引き、そのうえで（　）内の動詞を正しい形に変えてみましょう。

1. The shipment will not (be:　　　　　　　　　) available for the next three weeks.

2. The city concert was (hold:　　　　　　　　) last month.

3. He has been (work:　　　　　　　　) so hard since last Monday.

4. Instructors are expected to (submit:　　　　　　　　) evaluation sheets by Monday, July 28.

5. She has (be:　　　　　　　　) out of Japan for nearly seven years.

Try!

次の文を読んで、空所に入る最も適切な選択肢を選びましょう。

⟳ CheckLink

> To: All employees
> From: Ethan Reid, Human Resources Director
> Date: July 1
> Title: Performance Reviews
>
> The annual summer performance reviews are now ------- for the next three
> **1.**
> weeks. -------. It is the best way to learn about areas that need
> **2.**
> improvement. Managers are expected to finish filling out their subordinates'
> evaluation sheets and ------- them by Monday, July 28.
> **3.**
>
> Please note that every manager will ------- the director of the department
> **4.**
> they belong to for their annual review between July 30 and August 4.
>
> If you have any questions about the review process, contact Ethan Reid at
> Human Resources.

1. (A) scheduling   (B) being scheduled   (C) being scheduling   (D) schedule

Ⓐ Ⓑ Ⓒ Ⓓ

2. (A) The employees enjoy performances at great prices.
(B) The employees find the latest movie's review at the seminar.
(C) Reviews are an important chance for employees.
(D) The manager will provide an annual management plan.

Ⓐ Ⓑ Ⓒ Ⓓ

3. (A) submitting   (B) submitted   (C) submit   (D) submission

Ⓐ Ⓑ Ⓒ Ⓓ

4. (A) meet   (B) met   (C) meeting   (D) had met

Ⓐ Ⓑ Ⓒ Ⓓ

英語の語順で読んで（「返り読み」をやめて）スピードアップ

「返り読み」とは、英文を後ろから前に訳していく読み方のことを指します。返り読みをしながら Part 7 の問題を解いていると、必要以上に時間がかかってしまいます。返り読みをやめるには、英語を語順のまま、前から理解していくトレーニングが効果的です。

次の文書を読んで、第 1 文目のように、意味の切れ目にスラッシュ（/）を入れてみましょう。

Memorandum

■ The company / will help / pay new employees' moving expenses.

■ The employee is responsible for: making all arrangements involved in the move, except for making initial contact with the moving company; providing receipts for expenses such as hotels, and car rental; and submitting the application form. —[1]—.

■ The company will pay up to 15 days temporary living expenses for the new employee and his or her family. —[2]—.

■ Household moving expenses paid by the company include charges for packing, transportation, insurance, and unpacking as well as storage. The moving company will bill the company directly.

■ All the receipts must be kept and attached to the submission form. —[3]—.

■ After the employee has started work, the new employee will be allowed to assist his or her family moving to the new location for up to three work days with pay. —[4]—.

Try!

左の文書に関する以下の設問に対して、最も適切な答えを選択肢から選びましょう。　🔄CheckLink

1. For whom was the memo probably written?

   (A) Event organizations　　　(B) New staff members

   (C) Potential clients　　　　　(D) Training managers

                                             Ⓐ　Ⓑ　Ⓒ　Ⓓ

2. What are the employees NOT responsible for?

   (A) Keeping all the receipts

   (B) Submitting the application form

   (C) Making initial contact with the moving company

   (D) Providing the receipts for hotel expenses

                                             Ⓐ　Ⓑ　Ⓒ　Ⓓ

3. What should be attached to the submission form?

   (A) The new address　　　　　(B) The maximum allowance

   (C) The new employee's name　(D) All the receipts

                                             Ⓐ　Ⓑ　Ⓒ　Ⓓ

4. In which of the positions marked [1], [2], [3], and [4], does the following sentence best belong?

   "The maximum allowance is $80 per day."

   (A) [1]　　　　(B) [2]　　　　(C) [3]　　　　(D) [4]

                                             Ⓐ　Ⓑ　Ⓒ　Ⓓ

Review! **Unit 5**

☐ TOEIC では、(¹.　　　　) や (².　　　　) に関連した語句が頻出する。

☐ 上記の語句は、置かれている環境や使っている人物の (³.　　　) とともに覚えるとよい。

☐ トピックとしては、(⁴.　　　) との予約、オフィスにある (⁵.　　　) の故障などに関するものが多く取り上げられる。

☐ Part 6 では、空所の (⁶.　　　) をチェックすることによって (⁷.　　　) が特定できることがある。

☐ 「(⁸.　　　)」とは、英文を後ろから前に訳していくような読み方のことで、できれば避けたい読み方。(⁹.　　　) のまま、(¹⁰.　　　) 理解していく読み方のほうが効率的。

Build Up Your TOEIC Vocabulary!

At the Office 1

単語を覚えて、30秒以内にいくつ言えるか、ペアで確認してみましょう。

手順

① 英単語を見て意味を言う役とチェックする役に分かれて、お互いの教科書を交換する。
② 英単語を見て意味を言う役は、日本語訳を筆箱などで隠す。
③ 教員の合図とともに、1〜20の英単語を見て意味を言う（わからない場合は Let me skip it! と相手に伝えましょう）。
④ チェック役は相手の答えを聞き、正解していたら日本語訳の □ ボックスに左端から✓を入れる。
⑤ 同じ手順を日本語訳→英単語でも行う。

🎧 DL 070　💿 CD1-71

1. □□□ photocopier	1. □□□ コピー機
2. □□□ organize	2. □□□ 計画する、手配する
3. □□□ business trip	3. □□□ 出張
4. □□□ appointment	4. □□□ （人と会う）約束
5. □□□ document	5. □□□ 書類
6. □□□ invoice	6. □□□ 送り状、請求書
7. □□□ receptionist	7. □□□ 受付係
8. □□□ office supplies	8. □□□ 事務用品
9. □□□ business card	9. □□□ 名刺
10. □□□ retire	10. □□□ 退職する
11. □□□ staple	11. □□□ ホチキスでとめる
12. □□□ bulletin board	12. □□□ 掲示板
13. □□□ call back	13. □□□ 電話をかけ直す
14. □□□ attend	14. □□□ （会議に）出席する
15. □□□ equipment	15. □□□ 設備、装置
16. □□□ workplace	16. □□□ 職場
17. □□□ swipe	17. □□□ （カードを）機械に通す
18. □□□ promotion	18. □□□ 昇進、販売促進
19. □□□ contribute	19. □□□ 貢献する
20. □□□ available	20. □□□ 手があいている

＊点線のところで折ると活動がしやすくなります。

Unit 6 At the Office 2

TOEIC Part 1 写真描写問題

LISTENING Check Point!

3 人 以 上 の 写 真 は 状 況 に 要 注 意

Part 1 では、写真の中に複数の人間がいる場合、個々の動作よりも、全体の状況を問う問題が出題される傾向にあります。その際、写真の内容を深読みしすぎないように注意しましょう。

Practice!

写真を参考にして、空所の語句を聞き取ってみましょう。

🎧 DL 071 ~ 072　◉ CD2-02 ~ ◉ CD2-03

1.

2.

1. They're _____ _____ _____ .

2. Some people are _____ _____ _____ .

Try!

下の写真に関する英文が 4 つ読まれます。写真を最も適切に描写している選択肢を選びましょう。

↻ CheckLink　🎧 DL 073 ~ 074　◉ CD2-04 ~ ◉ CD2-05

1.

Ⓐ Ⓑ Ⓒ Ⓓ

2.

Ⓐ Ⓑ Ⓒ Ⓓ

TOEIC Part 4　説明文問題

短いスピーチを聞くポイントをマスターしよう

　Part 4 では、短いスピーチも多く出題されます。スピーチ形式の問題では、「誰に向けてのスピーチか」「何のためのスピーチか」、そして「（話し手または聞き手の）スピーチ終了後の行動」を聞き取ることが大切です。

 **Practice!**

次のスピーチの一節を読み、その目的を選択肢から選びましょう。　🔁 CheckLink

1. After a toast, please proceed to Room B for dinner. 　　　　[　]
2. Today, I am very happy to talk to you, new employees of this company. [　]
3. I'm here to inform you that we've got an excellent book review from *Monthly Business Journal*. 　　　　[　]

(A) 誰に向けてのスピーチか　　(B) 何のためのスピーチか　　(C) スピーチ終了後の行動

Try!

説明文を聞き、以下の設問に対して最も適切な答えを選択肢から選びましょう。

🔁 CheckLink　🎧 DL 075 ~ 078　◉ CD2-06 ~ ◉ CD2-09

1. Who most likely are the listeners?
   (A) Customers
   (B) Shareholders
   (C) New employees
   (D) Retired employees

　　　　　　Ⓐ Ⓑ Ⓒ Ⓓ

2. What is going to be held before lunch?
   (A) Explanation of a leading project
   (B) Introduction of new staff
   (C) Introduction of the new research team
   (D) A photo shoot for all staff members

　　　　　　Ⓐ Ⓑ Ⓒ Ⓓ

3. Why does the speaker say, "Would you look up at the screen there, please"?
   (A) To show new merchandise　　　(B) To introduce the presenter
   (C) To show their leading project　　(D) To make a video

　　　　　　Ⓐ Ⓑ Ⓒ Ⓓ

Improve Your TOEIC Listening Skills!

Part 4

TOEIC Part 4 形式の音声を聞き、以下の空所を埋めましょう。1回目は通常のスピードで、2回目はポーズ入りの音声が流れます。

※各空所はすべて正解した場合に、(〜〜〜) は3点、(＿＿) は2点、(＿＿) は1点として採点します（部分点はありません）。

🎧 DL 079 ~ 080　◎ CD2-10 ~ ◎ CD2-11

Hi, Terry. This is Lance. I want to (¹.〜〜〜〜〜〜〜〜〜〜) a few things before the (². ＿＿＿ ＿＿＿) on Friday. First of all, I'd like to (³.〜〜〜〜〜〜〜〜〜〜〜〜〜〜) at your production analysis before you present it to the meeting. I just want to check some of the (⁴. ＿＿＿) you've calculated. Also, I'd like to (⁵.〜〜〜〜〜〜〜〜〜〜) that there are no problems with the reports that you plan to (⁶. ＿＿＿ ＿＿＿) to the board members. I wish I (⁷. ＿＿＿) attend, but I can't leave Beijing until I close the (⁸. ＿＿＿). Anyway, I will (⁹. ＿＿＿ ＿＿＿) by next Monday. (¹⁰. ＿＿＿ ＿＿＿) soon.

上の伝言に関する以下の設問に対して、最も適切な答えを選択肢から選びましょう。 🔁 CheckLink

1. What is the purpose of this message?
(A) To inform a co-worker where the meeting will be held
(B) To help a co-worker write the annual report
(C) To cancel the meeting
(D) To give a co-worker some instructions

Ⓐ Ⓑ Ⓒ Ⓓ

2. What does Lance want Terry to do?
(A) Ask some questions　　(B) Postpone the board meeting
(C) Go to Beijing on a business trip　　(D) Prepare a copy of reports

Ⓐ Ⓑ Ⓒ Ⓓ

3. Why can't Lance leave Beijing?
(A) He needs to make an agreement with the client.
(B) He needs to say goodbye to the client.
(C) He needs to print out some copies.
(D) He needs to attend another board meeting.

Ⓐ Ⓑ Ⓒ Ⓓ

| Dictation Score | /20 |

名詞の可算・不可算を区別しよう

名詞には数えられるもの（可算名詞）と数えられないもの（不可算名詞）があります。前者は many、a lot of、a few、few などを使って数を表します。後者は much、a little、little などを使って量を表します。

可算名詞に使われるもの

> 例　many, a lot of, a few, few, quite a few, a great number of, the majority of

不可算名詞に使われるもの

> 例　much, a lot of, a little, little, a piece of

◆Practice!

[　] 内から正しい語句を選び、文を完成させましょう。　⟲CheckLink

1. My boss reads [(A) many / (B) much] books every month.

2. Do you have [(A) a lot of / (B) a few] work at hand now?

3. How [(A) many / (B) much] employees are there in your company?

4. My colleagues gave me [(A) a piece of / (B) a few] advice.

Try!

空所に入る語句として最も適切な選択肢を選び、文を完成させましょう。　⟲CheckLink

1. There are only ------- candidates left for the new position.
(Λ) much 　 (B) many 　 (C) a few 　 (D) little

Ⓐ Ⓑ Ⓒ Ⓓ

2. A great ------- of inquiries about our new product have come in recently.
(A) number 　 (B) figure 　 (C) piece 　 (D) amount

Ⓐ Ⓑ Ⓒ Ⓓ

3. Only ------- food has been prepared for the reception.
(A) a little 　 (B) a few 　 (C) few 　 (D) little

Ⓐ Ⓑ Ⓒ Ⓓ

4. Our company has had quite a ------- orders for the new product.

(A) little　(B) much　(C) some　(D) few

Ⓐ　Ⓑ　Ⓒ　Ⓓ

5. World Agency Corporation expects a large ------- of profit for this quarter.

(A) amount　(B) level　(C) piece　(D) deals

Ⓐ　Ⓑ　Ⓒ　Ⓓ

6. Tammy McCarthy, an economic analyst, is giving us ------- advice regarding successful marketing strategies.

(A) a lot　(B) a piece of　(C) many　(D) a few

Ⓐ　Ⓑ　Ⓒ　Ⓓ

7. The ------- of employees will get a pay raise thanks to the increase in our sales.

(A) majority　(B) most　(C) many　(D) amount

Ⓐ　Ⓑ　Ⓒ　Ⓓ

8. The Royal Service Company announced some news that caused -------- disappointment among stockholders.

(A) a few　(B) little　(C) many　(D) much

Ⓐ　Ⓑ　Ⓒ　Ⓓ

9. Only ------- knowledge is required to operate the new machinery.

(A) a few　(B) little　(C) a little　(D) few

Ⓐ　Ⓑ　Ⓒ　Ⓓ

10. We do not have ------- information on the policies recently decided by our new boss.

(A) much　(B) many　(C) a few　(D) few

Ⓐ　Ⓑ　Ⓒ　Ⓓ

状 況 を 読 み 取 ろ う

　英語でのオンライン（チャット）コミュニケーションは一見難しそうに見えますが、口語でのやりとりなので、あまり難しい語彙が使われない傾向にあります。この形式の攻略方法としては、やりとりが発生している状況を読み取ることが効果的です。具体的には、「登場人物の役割や間柄」や「何のためにチャットをしているか」といった状況を読み取るように心がけるとよいでしょう。

Practice!

次のチャットを読んで、やりとりの状況を読み取ってみましょう。

1. 登場人物（Anne, Tony, Maria）がそれぞれどこにいるか推測して、名前を入れてみましょう。

オフィス（　　　　　　　）　　オリエンテーション会場（　　　　　　　）　　社外（　　　　　　　）

2. チャットの目的として最もふさわしい選択肢を選びましょう。
(A) オリエンテーションの進捗状況の報告
(B) ランチョンセッションに誰が参加するか
(C) Anne が忘れ物をしてしまった

Anne Burns [11:36 A.M.]: I've just finished my part at the new employee orientation.

Tony Decker [11:38 A.M.]: How did it go?

Anne Burns [11:39 A.M.]: I was nervous since this was the first time that I had done it. But Ms. Johnson gave me her slides that she used last year, and it helped me a lot.

Maria Sato [11:41 A.M.]: That's nice. You should buy her several cups of coffee as a token of thanks when she returns from her maternity leave. Well, should I also join the luncheon session?

Anne Burns [11:42 A.M.]: Actually, if you have time, please. Some of the new employees seem to be interested in your research project.

Maria Sato [11:43 A.M.]: OK! See you soon!

Maria Sato [11:45 A.M.]: Sorry!! I just got the phone call from my boss. And he wants to see me before the meeting starts. Tony, could you join instead?

Tony Decker [11:46 A.M.]: Well, I'm still outside the company, but I think I will get there in 15 minutes.

Anne Burns [11:47 A.M.]: Good! Thank you!

Maria Sato [11:48 A.M.]: Please let me know if you find someone suitable for our project team.

Tony Decker [11:49 A.M.]: I will.

Anne Burns [11:50 A.M.]: Can I ask you a favor? Since more current employees are coming too, could you bring some name tags with you just in case?

Tony Decker [11:52 A.M.]: OK, no problem.

Try!

左の文書に関する以下の設問に対して、最も適当な答えを選択肢から選びましょう。　↻CheckLink

1. At 11:39 A.M., what does Ms. Burns indicate?

(A) She is organizing the orientation.

(B) It was the first time that she had given a talk at the orientation.

(C) She could not prepare for the presentation.

(D) She got some advice from her boss.

Ⓐ　Ⓑ　Ⓒ　Ⓓ

2. Which is most likely true of Ms. Johnson?

(A) She used to work with Ms. Burns at the same department.

(B) She is having another baby.

(C) She gave a talk last year at the orientation.

(D) She is the manager of the sales department.

Ⓐ　Ⓑ　Ⓒ　Ⓓ

3. Where do Ms. Sato and Mr. Decker probably work?

(A) A sales department　　(B) A marketing department

(C) A personnel department　　(D) A research department

Ⓐ　Ⓑ　Ⓒ　Ⓓ

4. At 11:49 A.M., what does Mr. Decker imply by writing, "I will"?

(A) He will bring some name tags for the luncheon session.

(B) He will have an interview for the project team.

(C) He will tell Ms. Sato if he finds someone good for the project.

(D) He will see the boss before the meeting instead of Ms. Burns.

Ⓐ　Ⓑ　Ⓒ　Ⓓ

Review! **Unit 6**

□ Part 1 では、写真の中に複数の人物がいる場合、(¹.　　　　) よりも、
(².　　　　) を問う問題がよく出題される。

□ Part 4 では、(³.　　　　) も多く出題される。その問題では、
「(⁴.　　　　)」「(⁵.　　　　)」、そして「(⁶.　　　　)」を聞き取ることが
大切。

□ 名詞には、「数えられるもの (⁷.　　　　)」と「数えられないもの
(⁸.　　　　)」がある。(⁹.　　　　) などは不可算名詞の修飾にのみ用いる。

□ Part 7 では、(¹⁰.　　　　) に関する問題も多く出題される。

Build Up Your TOEIC Vocabulary!

At the Office 2

単語を覚えて、30秒以内にいくつ言えるか、ペアで確認してみましょう。

手順

① 英単語を見て意味を言う役とチェックする役に分かれて、お互いの教科書を交換する。
② 英単語を見て意味を言う役は、日本語訳を筆箱などで隠す。
③ 教員の合図とともに、1～20の英単語を見て意味を言う（わからない場合は Let me skip it! と相手に伝えましょう）。
④ チェック役は相手の答えを聞き、正解していたら日本語訳の □ ボックスに左端から✓を入れる。
⑤ 同じ手順を日本語訳→英単語でも行う。

DL 081　CD2-12

1.	board of directors	1.	取締役会
2.	president	2.	社長
3.	stockholder	3.	株主
4.	quarter	4.	四半期
5.	inquiry	5.	問い合わせ、引き合い
6.	profit	6.	利益
7.	boss	7.	上司
8.	subordinate	8.	部下
9.	colleague	9.	同僚
10.	merger	10.	合併
11.	head office	11.	本社
12.	branch (office)	12.	支店
13.	department	13.	部
14.	section	14.	課
15.	general affairs department	15.	総務部
16.	sales department	16.	営業部
17.	accounting department	17.	経理部
18.	market share	18.	市場占有率
19.	public relations	19.	広報活動
20.	competitor	20.	競合他社

＊点線のところで折ると活動がしやすくなります。

Review Test 1

Part 1

下の写真に関する英文が4つ読まれます。写真を最も適切に描写しているものを選択肢から選びましょう。

CheckLink　◎ CD2-13　~　◎ CD2-16

1.

Ⓐ Ⓑ Ⓒ Ⓓ

2.

Ⓐ Ⓑ Ⓒ Ⓓ

3.

Ⓐ Ⓑ Ⓒ Ⓓ

4.

Ⓐ Ⓑ Ⓒ Ⓓ

/4

Part 2

質問文を聞き、最も適切な答えを選択肢から選びましょう。

CheckLink　◎ CD2-17　~　◎ CD2-23

5. Mark your answer on your answer sheet.　Ⓐ Ⓑ Ⓒ

6. Mark your answer on your answer sheet.　Ⓐ Ⓑ Ⓒ

7. Mark your answer on your answer sheet.　Ⓐ Ⓑ Ⓒ

8. Mark your answer on your answer sheet.　Ⓐ Ⓑ Ⓒ

9. Mark your answer on your answer sheet.　Ⓐ Ⓑ Ⓒ

10. Mark your answer on your answer sheet.　Ⓐ Ⓑ Ⓒ

11. Mark your answer on your answer sheet.　Ⓐ Ⓑ Ⓒ

/7

Part 3

会話を聞き、以下の設問に対して最も適切な答えを選択肢から選びましょう。

CheckLink CD2-24 ~ CD2-27

Happy Queen Supermarket

Strawberries·············Buy one package, Get one package FREE
Save $3.79 with card

Blackberries·············· 4 packages for $5
Avocados················· 10 packages for $10
Kiwi fruit················· 5 packages for $1

---

12. Who most likely is the woman?

(A) A restaurant owner   (B) A supermarket employee

(C) A newspaper reader   (D) A TV reporter

Ⓐ Ⓑ Ⓒ Ⓓ

13. Look at the graphic. Which items have an incorrect price tag?

(A) Strawberries   (B) Blackberries   (C) Avocados   (D) Kiwi fruit

Ⓐ Ⓑ Ⓒ Ⓓ

14. What does the woman say she will do next?

(A) Speak with a manager   (B) Call a newspaper publisher

(C) Correct the price sign   (D) Discount the item

Ⓐ Ⓑ Ⓒ Ⓓ

CheckLink CD2-28 ~ CD2-31

15. What is the man doing?

(A) He is reserving a room.   (B) He is cancelling the reservation.

(C) He is explaining the delay.   (D) He is taking a picture.

Ⓐ Ⓑ Ⓒ Ⓓ

16. What equipment does the meeting need?

(A) A TV monitor   (B) A whiteboard

(C) A big screen   (D) A computer

Ⓐ Ⓑ Ⓒ Ⓓ

17. Why does the man say, "Thank you for your offer, but I'm OK"?

(A) He needs to book a room as soon as possible.

(B) He thinks her offer does not meet his requirements.

(C) He thinks her offer is a wonderful one.

(D) He needs to have a smaller room for a meeting.

Ⓐ Ⓑ Ⓒ Ⓓ

/6

Part 4

説明文を聞き、以下の設問に対して最も適切な答えを選択肢から選びましょう。

CheckLink ⊙ CD2-32 ~ ⊙ CD2-35

18. Why has the express train been cancelled?

(A) Due to a mechanical problem (B) Due to heavy snow

(C) Due to an accident (D) Due to thick fog

Ⓐ Ⓑ Ⓒ Ⓓ

19. Where should the passengers go to make a new reservation?

(A) To the airport (B) To the ticket counter

(C) To the platform (D) To the check-in counter

Ⓐ Ⓑ Ⓒ Ⓓ

20. What will the passengers get by submitting the invalid tickets?

(A) A thorough explanation (B) Compensation

(C) Priority reservation (D) Cancellation

Ⓐ Ⓑ Ⓒ Ⓓ

CheckLink ⊙ CD2-36 ~ ⊙ CD2-39

Yoga Class Schedule		
	Studio A	**Studio B**
9:00 A.M.	Power Yoga	Power Yoga for Advanced
10:30 A.M.	Yoga Basic	Yoga Beginner

21. Look at the graphic. Which class did the speaker plan to take originally?

(A) Power Yoga (B) Power Yoga for advanced

(C) Yoga Basic (D) Yoga Beginner

Ⓐ Ⓑ Ⓒ Ⓓ

22. Why is the speaker going to the Mexican restaurant?

(A) She has a coupon. (B) It is near the yoga studio.

(C) The food is delicious. (D) The chef is her friend.

Ⓐ Ⓑ Ⓒ Ⓓ

23. What does the speaker offer to do?

(A) Pay for the meal (B) Make a reservation

(C) Call the yoga instructor (D) Respond to an e-mail

Ⓐ Ⓑ Ⓒ Ⓓ

/6

Part 5

空所に入る語句として最も適切な選択肢を選び、文を完成させましょう。　　🔁CheckLink

24. ------- knows the real price of the T-shirt that he bought.

(A) Everything　　(B) All　　(C) Anything　　(D) Everybody

Ⓐ　Ⓑ　Ⓒ　Ⓓ

25. The restaurant offers ------- higher quality food than the one across the street does.

(A) ever　　(B) little　　(C) further　　(D) much

Ⓐ　Ⓑ　Ⓒ　Ⓓ

26. Some people like to see soccer games at stadiums; ------- prefer watching them on TV.

(A) other　　(B) others　　(C) anyone　　(D) everyone

Ⓐ　Ⓑ　Ⓒ　Ⓓ

27. The company I work for has had quite a ------- orders for the new product.

(A) little　　(B) much　　(C) few　　(D) some

Ⓐ　Ⓑ　Ⓒ　Ⓓ

28. We do not have ------- information on the monetary policies recently decided by our government.

(A) much　　(B) many　　(C) a few　　(D) few

Ⓐ　Ⓑ　Ⓒ　Ⓓ

29. Membership of the Golden Fitness Club ------- two years from the day of issue.

(A) expiration　　(B) expiring　　(C) to expire　　(D) expires

Ⓐ　Ⓑ　Ⓒ　Ⓓ

30. The construction of the new building will ------- in July if everything goes smoothly.

(A) be completed　　(B) complete　　(C) be completing　　(D) completion

Ⓐ　Ⓑ　Ⓒ　Ⓓ

31. The application form must be ------- to Ms. Brown by this weekend.

(A) submit　　(B) submits　　(C) submitted　　(D) submitting

Ⓐ　Ⓑ　Ⓒ　Ⓓ

32. Please complete this customer satisfaction survey, and send ------- back to the office no later than April 13.

(A) you　　(B) them　　(C) it　　(D) us

Ⓐ　Ⓑ　Ⓒ　Ⓓ

33. The ------- model, QJ-5, is very popular among young people as this is the most recent.
(A) later   (B) latest   (C) latter   (D) lasted

Ⓐ Ⓑ Ⓒ Ⓓ

34. This is the kind of position ------- I have been seeking for a long time.
(A) whose   (B) that   (C) who   (D) whom

Ⓐ Ⓑ Ⓒ Ⓓ

35. The manufacturing of the new product was ------- due to the lack of raw materials.
(A) demanded   (B) delayed   (C) designed   (D) demonstrated

Ⓐ Ⓑ Ⓒ Ⓓ

36. ------- applicants must have a Ph.D. degree in psychology.
(A) By qualifying   (B) In qualified   (C) Qualified   (D) Qualifying

Ⓐ Ⓑ Ⓒ Ⓓ

╱13

Part 6

次の文を読み、空所に入る語句として最も適切な選択肢を選びましょう。　 CheckLink

Notice of Construction Work

The Central Subway Project will begin drilling operations for a supplemental geotechnical ------- in your neighborhood. From March 10-15, drilling will take
37.
place on Fourth and Sixth Streets. -------.
38.

Please review the ------- file for more information regarding the construction
39.
work hours and duration of these drilling operations. If you have any questions or concerns, please contact us. We appreciate your cooperation and -------.
40.

---

37. (A) investigating
    (B) investigate
    (C) investigated
    (D) investigation

Ⓐ Ⓑ Ⓒ Ⓓ

38. (A) The manager can answer the questions about the service.
    (B) On March 16th, the parade will be held.
    (C) We sincerely apologize for any inconvenience this may cause.
    (D) The government regulation plays a key role in ensuring safe construction.

Ⓐ Ⓑ Ⓒ Ⓓ

39. (A) attaching
    (B) attach
    (C) attachment
    (D) attached

Ⓐ Ⓑ Ⓒ Ⓓ

40. (A) understand
    (B) understood
    (C) understanding
    (D) understands

Ⓐ Ⓑ Ⓒ Ⓓ

／4

Part 7

次の文書を読み、設問に対して最も適切な答えを選択肢から選びましょう。

 CheckLink

Scott Ortiz [2:50 P.M.]: Where are you now? The staff meeting is about to start! Everyone except you seems to be already in the meeting room.

Ralph Kramer [2:52 P.M.]: Sorry, I'm on my way now. I'm stuck in traffic at the moment. It looks like I can't make it there until around three. Megan, can you switch the order of the presentation?

Megan Foster [2:53 P.M.]: It's okay but I need to pick up the document for my presentation before that.

Scott Ortiz [2:54 P.M.]: I could do that for you. Who should I ask at the sales department?

Megan Foster [2:54 P.M.]: Ms. Smith is arranging all the documents I need. As you know, she wears glasses and has long brown hair. Her desk is near the copying machine.

Scott Ortiz [2:55 P.M.]: Thank you for the information. I'll get you the document.

Megan Foster [2:56 P.M.]: Thank you! Is there anything I can help you with, Ralph?

Ralph Kramer [2:57 P.M.]: Well, just one thing. I'm wondering if my handouts have been printed out.

Megan Foster [2:58 P.M.]: John is distributing them to the staff now. Are there any problems?

Ralph Kramer [2:59 P.M.]: Actually, I wanted to double-check the numbers which John fixed this morning before the meeting. Could you send me a picture of it, then?

---

41. At 2:54 P.M., what does Mr. Ortiz indicate?

(A) He has never worked with Ms. Foster.

(B) He is attending the meeting as well.

(C) Ms. Smith has just started to work.

(D) He is not working at the sales department. Ⓐ Ⓑ Ⓒ Ⓓ

42. What is implied about John?

(A) He is in charge of the project.

(B) He fixed the copying machine.

(C) He gives the presentation at the meeting.

(D) He modified the handout before the meeting. Ⓐ Ⓑ Ⓒ Ⓓ

次の文書を読み、設問に対して最も適切な答えを選択肢から選びましょう。　⟳CheckLink

From:	Linda Tucker
To:	Mr. Oliver L. Farnell
Subject:	Application
Date:	July, 15, 2021

Dear Mr. Farnell,

I saw your job opening for a sales manager in *Daily Today*, and I would like to apply for this position. —[1]—.

I have been a sales manager for a furniture import company for the last five years. —[2]—. I was also in charge of the international sales department. —[3]—.

Attached to this email is a copy of my résumé for your consideration.

I look forward to hearing from you soon. —[4]—.

Sincerely,

Linda Tucker

43. What is the purpose of the email?
(A) To offer a position
(B) To submit a sales report
(C) To apply for a job
(D) To report trouble

Ⓐ　Ⓑ　Ⓒ　Ⓓ

44. What does Ms. Tucker send with the email?
(A) Her complete shopping list
(B) Her new business plan
(C) Her job application essay
(D) Her work background information

Ⓐ　Ⓑ　Ⓒ　Ⓓ

45. In which of the positions marked [1], [2], [3], and [4], does the following sentence best belong?

"I believe my experience and background will help your company expand its business."

(A) [1]　　　　(B) [2]　　　　(C) [3]　　　　(D) [4]

Ⓐ　Ⓑ　Ⓒ　Ⓓ

Claiborne Road House For Sale!

This 2,067 square foot, three-bedroom, two-full bathroom, one-half bath house is for sale for only $135 dollars per square foot. Features include attached parking lots and central heating. The kitchen includes a dishwasher, a garbage disposal unit, and a microwave oven. If you need more details, send an email to Max Tremblay, our sales manager: max_homebuilder@realestate.com

From:	Naomi Stevenson <nao.stevenson05@pext.jp>
To:	Max Tremblay <max_homebuilder@realestate.com>
Subject:	Questions about the house

Dear Mr. Tremblay,

I'm writing to you regarding MD 21901 for sale on Claiborne Road. I'm very interested in it, but I have a few questions.

First, when was this property built? I'd like to buy something built within the past five years.

Second, according to the advertisement, there are two-full bathrooms and one-half bath. But, I don't know what exactly "half" means. Does it mean a shower room, or is it simply half the size of a normal bathroom? In that case, how big is it?

Could you also send details and photos of other highly recommended properties?

Looking forward to your reply. Thank you in advance.

Sincerely,

Naomi Stevenson

P.S.

I'm leaving for Turkey for a couple of weeks, so my reply might be late.

46. What is the purpose of the advertisement?

(A) To offer real estate agents an investment opportunity

(B) To inform the details of the renovated house

(C) To introduce a property to customers

(D) To describe the recent renovations

Ⓐ　Ⓑ　Ⓒ　Ⓓ

47. What is NOT described as the feature of the house?

(A) A garden

(B) A garbage disposal unit

(C) Parking lots

(D) A central heating system

Ⓐ　Ⓑ　Ⓒ　Ⓓ

48. What is Ms. Stevenson's requirement for the house?

(A) Safe and quiet neighborhood

(B) High quality equipment in the kitchen

(C) Relative newness of the property

(D) Full renovation of the bathrooms

Ⓐ　Ⓑ　Ⓒ　Ⓓ

49. What does Ms. Stevenson ask Mr. Tremblay to do?

(A) To call her back soon

(B) To give her some other recommendations

(C) To give her a discount

(D) To make a reservation for a tour of the house

Ⓐ　Ⓑ　Ⓒ　Ⓓ

50. Why is Ms. Stevenson unable to reply to Mr. Tremblay soon?

(A) Her computer has been broken.

(B) She will be out of the country.

(C) She will be moving to a new location.

(D) She will be in hospital for some treatment.

Ⓐ　Ⓑ　Ⓒ　Ⓓ

╱10

| Total | ╱50 |

Doing Business Online

TOEIC Part 1
写真描写問題

LISTENING Check Point!

言 い か え 表 現 に 気 を つ け よ う ①

Part 1 では、写真内にある名詞が通常の表現とは違う言い方で述べられている場合があります。例えば、cake や coffee などが snack や refreshments という表現に言いかえられたりします。その他にも、PC や smartphone が device となったりすることも多いので注意が必要です。

Practice!

写真を参考にして、空所の語句を聞き取ってみましょう。

DL 082 ~ 083　　CD2-40　~　CD2-41

1.　　　　　　　　　　　　　　　　　**2.**

1. A woman is on _____ _____ .

2. The man is _____ _____ .

Try!

下の写真に関する英文が4つ読まれます。写真を最も適切に描写している選択肢を選びましょう。

CheckLink　DL 084 ~ 085　　CD2-42　~　CD2-43

1.

Ⓐ Ⓑ Ⓒ Ⓓ

2.

Ⓐ Ⓑ Ⓒ Ⓓ

How ではじまる疑問文を攻略しよう

Part 2 では、How ではじまる疑問文が多く出題されます。例えば、How far（距離）、How long（期間）、How about（提案）、How much（値段や量）、How soon（いつ）、How often（頻度）などです。これらに十分注意しましょう。

Practice!

以下の How ではじまる疑問文には、どのような答えが予想されるでしょうか。下の選択肢から最も適切なものを選びましょう。

CheckLink

1. How long is the warranty on this wireless keyboard? [   ]

2. How soon will the product arrive? [   ]

3. How about posting a message to that blog? [   ]

4. How often do you use online shopping? [   ]

5. How much does express delivery cost? [   ]

(A) That's a good idea.　(B) $20　(C) It depends.
(D) Once in a week　(E) 3 years

Try!

質問文を聞き、最も適切な答えを選択肢から選びましょう。

CheckLink　DL 086 ~ 090　CD2-44 ~ CD2-48

1. Mark your answer on your answer sheet.　Ⓐ Ⓑ Ⓒ

2. Mark your answer on your answer sheet.　Ⓐ Ⓑ Ⓒ

3. Mark your answer on your answer sheet.　Ⓐ Ⓑ Ⓒ

4. Mark your answer on your answer sheet.　Ⓐ Ⓑ Ⓒ

5. Mark your answer on your answer sheet.　Ⓐ Ⓑ Ⓒ

Improve Your TOEIC Listening Skills!

Part 1 & Part 2

TOEIC Part 1 および Part 2 形式の音声を聞き、以下の空所を埋めましょう。1回目は通常のスピードで、2回目はポーズ入りの音声が流れます。その後、1に関しては写真を最もよく描写しているものを、2および3に関しては質問文に対する最も適切な答えを選択肢から選びましょう。

※各空所はすべて正解した場合に、(＿＿＿) は3点、(＿＿＿) は2点、(＿＿＿) は1点として採点します（部分点はありません）。

1.

CheckLink DL 091 ~ 092   CD2-49 ~ CD2-50

(A) A man is (¹.＿＿＿＿＿＿＿) the stock.

(B) A man is (².＿＿＿＿＿＿＿) coffee.

(C) A man is (³.＿＿＿＿＿＿＿) a watch.

(D) A man is (⁴.＿＿＿＿＿＿＿＿＿
＿＿＿＿＿＿＿＿＿＿＿＿＿).

Ⓐ Ⓑ Ⓒ Ⓓ

CheckLink DL 093 ~ 094   CD2-51 ~ CD2-52

2. Why did you change the mobile application design?

(A) In (¹.＿＿＿＿＿)

(B) Well, (².＿＿＿＿＿＿＿＿＿) was unfavorable.

(C) I think (³.＿＿＿＿＿ ＿＿＿＿＿ ＿＿＿＿＿) $50.

Ⓐ Ⓑ Ⓒ

CheckLink DL 095 ~ 096   CD2-53 ~ CD2-54

3. We're going to be really busy this month, (¹.＿＿＿＿＿＿＿＿＿＿＿)?

(A) (².＿＿＿＿＿＿＿＿＿＿＿＿＿＿).

(B) Our homepage has been (³.＿＿＿＿＿＿).

(C) No, the (⁴.＿＿＿＿＿) isn't here.

Ⓐ Ⓑ Ⓒ

Dictation Score　／20

TOEIC Part **5** 短文穴埋め問題

仮 定 法 の 基 本 を 理 解 し よ う

　仮定法とは、ある事柄を事実としてではなく、想像、願望などの立場から述べる言い方です。現在の事実に反する仮定には過去形（be 動詞はつねに were）、過去の事実に反する仮定には過去完了形（had＋過去分詞）を用います。

　また、wish と一緒に過去形や過去完了形を用いて願望を表現することもできます。

> 例　現在に反する例：If I *were* a rich man, I *would* buy the car.
>
> 　　過去に反する例：If I *had been* a rich man, I *would have* bought the car.
>
> 　　現在の実現が困難な願望の例：I wish I *had* more money.
>
> 　　過去に実現しなかった願望の例：I wish they *had come* to the party.

 **Practice!**

[　] 内から正しい語句を選び、文を完成させましょう。　　　　ＣＣheckLink

1. If I [(A) had / (B) had had] more money, I could start my own company.

2. If they [(A) were / (B) had been] more careful, they wouldn't have lost money.

3. I wish I [(A) had left / (B) left] before the typhoon stopped the train.

4. If you [(A) didn't open / (B) hadn't opened] the file, the computer wouldn't have got the virus.

 **Try!**

空所に入る語句として最も適切な選択肢を選び、文を完成させましょう。　　ＣＣheckLink

1. I wouldn't have started an online business if I ------- that magazine article by chance.

(A) hadn't read　　(B) didn't read　　(C) don't read　　(D) am not reading

Ⓐ　Ⓑ　Ⓒ　Ⓓ

2. If your computer ------- antivirus software, you could have a big problem.

(A) weren't　　(B) wasn't　　(C) didn't have　　(D) hadn't had

Ⓐ　Ⓑ　Ⓒ　Ⓓ

3. If the Internet didn't exist, it ------- impossible to reach so many customers around the world.

(A) would be   (B) could have been   (C) had been   (D) were

Ⓐ Ⓑ Ⓒ Ⓓ

4. If this website were designed more elegantly, it ------- even more online customers.

(A) attracts   (B) were attracting   (C) had attracted   (D) could attract

Ⓐ Ⓑ Ⓒ Ⓓ

5. Our reputation ------- damaged if the product hadn't been delivered in time.

(A) could be   (B) has been   (C) could have been   (D) was

Ⓐ Ⓑ Ⓒ Ⓓ

6. If there weren't any risk of online fraud, people ------- orders on websites more comfortably.

(A) could place   (B) have placed   (C) could have placed   (D) placed

Ⓐ Ⓑ Ⓒ Ⓓ

7. I wish we ------- more staff members to handle the sudden increase of orders this month.

(A) have had   (B) were having   (C) had   (D) have

Ⓐ Ⓑ Ⓒ Ⓓ

8. If I hadn't asked him for help, it ------- much longer to design the current website.

(A) would take   (B) would have taken   (C) took   (D) has taken

Ⓐ Ⓑ Ⓒ Ⓓ

9. If we hadn't received the large order last month, we ------- out of business.

(A) went   (B) were going   (C) might go   (D) might have gone

Ⓐ Ⓑ Ⓒ Ⓓ

10. I wish the website designer ------- much less money for designing our company website.

(A) has charged   (B) had charged   (C) has been charging   (D) charges

Ⓐ Ⓑ Ⓒ Ⓓ

注 意 書 き を 見 落 と さ な い よ う に し よ う

　Part 7 では、本文中だけでなく、欄外や脚注、またはアスタリスク（＊）の後などに書かれている情報が問題として出題されることがあります。これらは小さな字で書かれていることが多いので、見落とさずに情報をおさえるようにしましょう。

次の文書に含まれている注意書きの情報に〇をつけてみましょう。また、どんな情報が書かれているか確認しましょう。

Intelligent Marketing & Customer Service
Use your smartphone on your business!

Your potential customers keep their cell phones with them 16 hours a day and look at their phone on average 150 times per day. The mobile wave is already here. Because texting is so personal, the messages you send have a big impact. Texting is the most effective channel available to engage your customers. As a service to customers, we have a live chat option to answer customers immediately on our website. So if you experience any difficulty in learning or using the powerful features in TextDay, please call our online service center!

FEATURES AND BENEFITS

■ Lowest Cost Text Marketing

■ Upload Existing Customer Lists

■ Unlimited Contact Groups

■ Automated Customer Service

＊ Detailed information is available upon request.

Downtown Office

1429 2nd St. Wington, CA 56982

(913) 435-6677

＊ Office hours are between 8:00 A.M. and 6:30 P.M.

Online Customer Service Center

textday.business.com

＊ Open between 8:30 A.M. and 5:00 P.M.

Try!

左の文書に関する以下の設問に対して、最も適切な答えを選択肢から選びましょう。 ⟲CheckLink

1. According to the advertisement, how many hours a week do people keep their cell phone with them?

(A) 100 hours　　(B) 112 hours　　(C) 128 hours　　(D) 144 hours

Ⓐ　Ⓑ　Ⓒ　Ⓓ

2. Why does texting have a big impact?

(A) It is personal.　　　　(B) It is interesting.

(C) It is available.　　　　(D) It is original.

Ⓐ　Ⓑ　Ⓒ　Ⓓ

3. How does the service staff respond to customers?

(A) By sending letters　　(B) By calling

(C) By email　　　　　　(D) By chatting online

Ⓐ　Ⓑ　Ⓒ　Ⓓ

4. What time is the online customer service available?

(A) 8:00 A.M.　　(B) 9:00 A.M.　　(C) 5:25 P.M.　　(D) 6:30 P.M.

Ⓐ　Ⓑ　Ⓒ　Ⓓ

Review!　Unit 8

☐ Part 1 では、名詞の (¹.　　　　　　　　) 表現に注意。

☐ Part 2 では、(².　　　　　　　　) ではじまる問題文が頻出する。例えば、(³.　　　　　　　　) なら距離を、(⁴.　　　　　　　　) なら時間を尋ねる問題となる。また、(⁵.　　　　　　　　) なら提案を表す。

☐ 仮定法では、現在の事実に反する仮定には (⁶.　　　　　　　　) が、過去の事実に反する仮定では (⁷.　　　　　　　　) が用いられる。

☐ Part 7 では、(⁸.　　　　　　　　) の情報を見落とさないように気をつける。これらの情報は (⁹.　　　　　　　　) にあったり、(¹⁰.　　　　　　　　) マーク付きで示されていることが多い。

Build Up Your TOEIC Vocabulary!

Doing Business Online

単語を覚えて、30秒以内にいくつ言えるか、ペアで確認してみましょう。

手順

① 英単語を見て意味を言う役とチェックする役に分かれて、お互いの教科書を交換する。

② 英単語を見て意味を言う役は、日本語訳を筆箱などで隠す。

③ 教員の合図とともに、1～20の英単語を見て意味を言う（わからない場合は Let me skip it! と相手に伝えましょう）。

④ チェック役は相手の答えを聞き、正解していたら日本語訳の □ ボックスに左端から✓を入れる。

⑤ 同じ手順を日本語訳→英単語でも行う。

🎧 DL 097　💿 CD2-55

1.	available	1.	入手可能な
2.	demand	2.	需要
3.	handle	3.	処理する
4.	item	4.	品目
5.	market	5.	市場
6.	order	6.	注文（する）
7.	payment	7.	支払い
8.	ship	8.	出荷する
9.	estimate	9.	見積り
10.	product	10.	製品
11.	purchase	11.	購入する
12.	shipping charges	12.	運送費用
13.	merchandise	13.	商品
14.	delivery	14.	配達
15.	advertise	15.	宣伝する
16.	customer	16.	顧客
17.	respond	17.	返答する
18.	export	18.	輸出する
19.	online fraud	19.	オンライン詐欺
20.	attached file	20.	添付ファイル

＊点線のところで折ると活動がしやすくなります。

TOEIC Part 1 写真描写問題

動 作 ・ 動 き を 表 す 表 現 に 注 意 し よ う ③

Part 1 では、以下のような動作に関する表現がよく出題されています。聞こえた瞬間にどのような動作を指しているのか理解できるようにくり返し練習しましょう。

load ... into a truck
（トラックに…を積みこむ）

reach out for ...
（…に手を伸ばす）

lean against the wall
（壁にもたれる）

◆ Practice!

写真を参考にして、空所の語句を聞き取ってみましょう。

DL 098 ～ 099   CD2-56 ～ CD2-57

1.

2.

1. A man is painting _____ _____ .

2. A man is _____ _____ _____ to a woman.

◆ Try!

下の写真に関する英文が 4 つ読まれます。写真を最も適切に描写している選択肢を選びましょう。

CheckLink   DL 100 ～ 101   CD2-58 ～ CD2-59

1.

Ⓐ Ⓑ Ⓒ Ⓓ

2.

Ⓐ Ⓑ Ⓒ Ⓓ

よ く 出 る 設 問 を お さ え よ う

Part 3 では、いくつか定番の設問があります。それらが何をたずねているのか、見たらすぐに理解できるよう覚えておきましょう。

Practice!

以下の設問がたずねている内容として最も適切なものを選択肢から1つ選びましょう。

CheckLink

1. What will the man probably do next? [　]
2. What does the woman ask for? [　]
3. What are the panelists discussing? [　]
4. What is wrong with the machine? [　]
5. What does the woman offer to do? [　]

(A) 申し出の内容　(B) 要求の内容　(C) 次の行動　(D) 問題点　(E) 話題

Try!

会話を聞き、以下の設問に対して最も適切な答えを選択肢から選びましょう。

CheckLink　DL 102 ~ 105　CD2-60 ~ CD2-63

1. What are the speakers mainly discussing?
　(A) Travel arrangements　(B) Delivery services
　(C) Packing for moving　(D) Renovating the room

Ⓐ　Ⓑ　Ⓒ　Ⓓ

2. What does the man suggest to the woman?
　(A) Make a priority list　(B) Start packing immediately
　(C) Go and see an expert　(D) Find your belongings

Ⓐ　Ⓑ　Ⓒ　Ⓓ

3. What does the man offer to do?
　(A) Clean his apartment　(B) Help packing for moving
　(C) Check the list　(D) Book a room at a hotel

Ⓐ　Ⓑ　Ⓒ　Ⓓ

Improve Your TOEIC Listening Skills!

TOEIC Part 3 形式の音声を聞き、以下の空所を埋めましょう。1 回目は通常のスピードで、2 回目はポーズ入りの音声が流れます。

※各空所はすべて正解した場合に、(＿＿＿) は 3 点、(＿＿＿) は 2 点、(＿＿＿) は 1 点として採点します（部分点はありません）。

🎧 DL 106 ~ 107　◎ CD2-64　~　◎ CD2-65

W: Hello. I checked your (1.＿＿＿＿ ＿＿＿＿) and liked your company's (2.＿＿＿＿). I just (3.＿＿＿＿ ＿＿＿＿) a new house and I'm interested in making (4.＿＿＿＿ ＿＿＿＿ ＿＿＿＿) to my yard.

M: I see. Do you have any (5.＿＿＿＿) image of your yard?

W: Not exactly. So, I'd like to meet the designer and talk about (6.＿＿＿＿ ＿＿＿＿ ＿＿＿＿) together.

M: Thank you, but our designer is currently (7.＿＿＿＿ ＿＿＿＿). Could you (8.＿＿＿＿) your name and number? I'll make sure he (9.＿＿＿＿ ＿＿＿＿ ＿＿＿＿) this afternoon (10.＿＿＿＿ ＿＿＿＿) the meeting schedule.

上の会話に関する以下の設問に対して、最も適切な答えを選択肢から選びましょう。　⟳ CheckLink

1. What does the woman want to do?
  (A) Remodel her yard   (B) Create her website
  (C) Design the house   (D) Take a vacation   Ⓐ Ⓑ Ⓒ Ⓓ

2. Why does the woman want to meet the designer?
  (A) To talk about the colors and designs
  (B) To talk about the designs and time
  (C) To talk about the designs and budget
  (D) To talk about the schedule and budget   Ⓐ Ⓑ Ⓒ Ⓓ

3. What will the designer probably do this afternoon?
  (A) Write a letter to the woman   (B) Send an email to the woman
  (C) Call the woman   (D) Meet the woman   Ⓐ Ⓑ Ⓒ Ⓓ

Dictation Score ／20

前 置 詞 の 基 本 イ メ ー ジ を つ か も う

　前置詞は名詞・代名詞の前で用いられ、場所や時間などを表します。前置詞には基本イメージがあり、これをおさえておくと様々な場面で応用が可能となります（p.15、Check Point! 参照）。

　なお、2語以上が一緒になって前置詞の働きをすることもよくあるので、これらはイディオムとして覚えておきましょう（例：because of、in front of）。

基本イメージの例

in：（取り囲まれて）中に入っているイメージ
There is a TV **in** the corner of the room.［隅に入り込んでいる感じ］

on：表面に接しているイメージ
There is a fly **on** the ceiling.［表面に接している感じ］

at：点や特定の場所のイメージ
Turn right **at** the next corner.［地図上の1点としてとらえている感じ］

◆Practice!

[　　] 内から正しい語句を選び、文を完成させましょう。　　🔗CheckLink

1. Our cat is sleeping [(A) under / (B) in] the table right now.

2. There is a good Italian restaurant [(A) across / (B) over] the street.

3. Let's meet here [(A) on / (B) at] 5 o'clock and go for dinner.

4. Our flight to Chicago was cancelled [(A) on / (B) because of] bad weather.

◆ Try!

空所に入る語句として最も適切な選択肢を選び、文を完成させましょう。　　🔗CheckLink

1. I am looking for an affordable house ------- a quiet residential area.
(A) on　　(B) in　　(C) to　　(D) during

Ⓐ　Ⓑ　Ⓒ　Ⓓ

2. This is a perfect property, close ------- the school and train station as well as the shopping mall.
(A) under　　(B) over　　(C) on　　(D) to

Ⓐ　Ⓑ　Ⓒ　Ⓓ

3. The real-estate agent is going to show us a couple of properties ------- 10:00.

(A) during (B) from (C) in (D) on

Ⓐ Ⓑ Ⓒ Ⓓ

4. We moved into a new house by the lake ------- July 12, 2021.

(A) from (B) in (C) on (D) at

Ⓐ Ⓑ Ⓒ Ⓓ

5. The neighborhood of the property looked completely different ------- the evening.

(A) in (B) to (C) at (D) under

Ⓐ Ⓑ Ⓒ Ⓓ

6. Maybe I should go to another real-estate agent ------- the street.

(A) above (B) over (C) between (D) across

Ⓐ Ⓑ Ⓒ Ⓓ

7. The keys to the entrance of our new house are ------- my purse.

(A) over (B) in (C) during (D) to

Ⓐ Ⓑ Ⓒ Ⓓ

8. There is a convenience store ------- the first floor of the building.

(A) on (B) in (C) over (D) because of

Ⓐ Ⓑ Ⓒ Ⓓ

9. We have to decide on the properties ------- the end of this month.

(A) across (B) under (C) on (D) by

Ⓐ Ⓑ Ⓒ Ⓓ

10. Although the apartment looks very nice, we will have to give up on renting it ------- the high rent.

(A) because of (B) in front of (C) to (D) from

Ⓐ Ⓑ Ⓒ Ⓓ

TOEIC Part 7 読解問題

用 紙 や 表 に 親 し も う

　Part 7 のダブルパッセージやトリプルパッセージでは、用紙や表が先に提示され、次にそれらに関連したパッセージが続くことがよくあります（その逆の場合もあります）。用紙や表の表現と構成をおさえて、その中にある情報を迷わず探せるようにしましょう。

Practice!

以下の語句に相当する日本語訳を選択肢から選びましょう。　　　　　　　　　CheckLink

1. Invoice 　　　　　　　　　　　　　　　　　　　　　　[　　]

2. Notice 　　　　　　　　　　　　　　　　　　　　　　[　　]

3. Customer Satisfaction Survey 　　　　　　　　　　　[　　]

4. Order Confirmation 　　　　　　　　　　　　　　　　[　　]

5. Itinerary 　　　　　　　　　　　　　　　　　　　　　[　　]

6. Application Form 　　　　　　　　　　　　　　　　　[　　]

(A) 送り状	(B) 申込書	(C) 注文確認書
(D) 顧客満足度調査	(E) お知らせ	(F) 旅程表

下の用紙と次のページの手紙をよく読んでみましょう。

Customer Satisfaction Survey

Thank you for using our company. To better serve our customers, we would like you to take a few minutes to complete this customer satisfaction survey.

	Strongly agree				Strongly disagree
Our staff explained the contract clearly.	5	—④—	3	— 2 —	1
Our staff had enough knowledge/skills.	5	— 4 —	③	— 2 —	1
You are satisfied with our website service.	5	— 4 —	3	—②—	1
HappyHome is convenient to use.	5	— 4 —	③	— 2 —	1
I would use *HappyHome* again in the future.	5	— 4 —	③	— 2 —	1

Do you have any additional comments about our company? Write here if any.

We are happy that we were able to buy a fabulous house within our budget, but there are several things that need to be improved by your company. First, your website is rarely updated. Actually, one of the excellent houses we found on your website had already been sold long before we visited your office. Also, we think the quality of your staff needs to be improved. Mr. Potter especially was often delayed for our meetings, even on the contract day. He is, we are afraid, unprofessional.

Customer's Name *Sato Hiroko*

Dear Ms. Sato,

Thank you very much for taking the time to complete our survey and for your feedback. We apologize for any inconvenience you went through. As for our website, it had been put on hold for renewal, but it is now open again, and you can find up-to-date information. If you find any further problems on our website, please let us know.

We also sincerely apologize that our staff member, Mr. Potter, caused you great trouble. He is clearly lacking in responsibility and his behavior is intolerable. We asked him to write an explanation letter about this matter, and made sure that he would never act like that again. Please accept a gift card enclosed as our token of apology.

Sincerely,

Charles Donovan

Charles Donovan
Senior Service Manager,
HappyHome Real Estate Agent

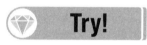 **Try!**

2つの文書に関する以下の設問に対して、最も適切な答えを選択肢から選びましょう。

⟲CheckLink

1. What can be inferred from the comments?
   (A) One employee is not professional.
   (B) All the employees are not professional.
   (C) Ms. Sato did not buy a house at *HappyHome*.
   (D) Ms. Sato was happy with the website.

Ⓐ Ⓑ Ⓒ Ⓓ

2. What is a complaint that Ms. Sato has about the company?
   (A) Location of the branch
   (B) Locations of the houses they are selling
   (C) Quality of the staff
   (D) Quality of the houses they are selling

Ⓐ Ⓑ Ⓒ Ⓓ

3. Why had the website not been updated?

(A) Due to bad Internet connection

(B) Due to a computer virus

(C) Due to website renewal

(D) Due to staff quality

Ⓐ　Ⓑ　Ⓒ　Ⓓ

4. What was Mr. Potter asked to do?

(A) To explain the trouble in writing

(B) To send a gift certificate to Ms. Sato

(C) To write a polite email

(D) To resign immediately

Ⓐ　Ⓑ　Ⓒ　Ⓓ

5. What is included with the letter?

(A) A souvenir

(B) A meal coupon

(C) A gift card

(D) A check

Ⓐ　Ⓑ　Ⓒ　Ⓓ

Review! **Unit 9**

☐ Part 1 では、(¹.　　　　　　　) に関する表現がよく出題される。

☐ Part 3 では、いくつか定番の (².　　　　　　) があるので、すべてを読まず
瞬時に反応できるようにしておくとよい。

☐ 前置詞は (³.　　　　　　) をおさえておくと様々な場面で応用が可能となる。
例えば、in なら (⁴.　　　　　　)、on なら (⁵.　　　　　　)、at なら
(⁶.　　　　　　) を持つとよい。

☐ 2語以上が一緒になって前置詞の働きをする (⁷.　　　　　) や
(⁸.　　　　　) などの表現に注意する。

☐ Part 7 のダブルパッセージやトリプルパッセージでは、文書に
(⁹.　　　　　) や (¹⁰.　　　　　　) を組み合わせたような出題も多い。

Build Up Your TOEIC Vocabulary!

Housing

単語を覚えて、30秒以内にいくつ言えるか、ペアで確認してみましょう。

手順

① 英単語を見て意味を言う役とチェックする役に分かれて、お互いの教科書を交換する。
② 英単語を見て意味を言う役は、日本語訳を筆箱などで隠す。
③ 教員の合図とともに、1〜20の英単語を見て意味を言う（わからない場合は Let me skip it! と相手に伝えましょう）。
④ チェック役は相手の答えを聞き、正解していたら日本語訳の □ ボックスに左端から✓を入れる。
⑤ 同じ手順を日本語訳→英単語でも行う。

🎧 DL 108　　◎ CD2-66

1. ☐☐☐ property	1. ☐☐☐ （不動産の）物件
2. ☐☐☐ location	2. ☐☐☐ 場所、位置
3. ☐☐☐ residential area	3. ☐☐☐ 住宅地
4. ☐☐☐ rent	4. ☐☐☐ 家賃
5. ☐☐☐ affordable	5. ☐☐☐ 手頃な
6. ☐☐☐ furnished	6. ☐☐☐ 家具付きの
7. ☐☐☐ (chest of) drawers	7. ☐☐☐ タンス
8. ☐☐☐ convenient	8. ☐☐☐ 便利な
9. ☐☐☐ condominium	9. ☐☐☐ 分譲マンション
10. ☐☐☐ landlord	10. ☐☐☐ 家主
11. ☐☐☐ (single) house	11. ☐☐☐ 一戸建て
12. ☐☐☐ studio apartment	12. ☐☐☐ ワンルームマンション
13. ☐☐☐ security deposit	13. ☐☐☐ 敷金
14. ☐☐☐ utilities	14. ☐☐☐ （電気・ガスなどの）公共料金
15. ☐☐☐ mortgage	15. ☐☐☐ 住宅ローン
16. ☐☐☐ furniture	16. ☐☐☐ 家具
17. ☐☐☐ real estate	17. ☐☐☐ 不動産
18. ☐☐☐ villa	18. ☐☐☐ 別荘
19. ☐☐☐ dining room	19. ☐☐☐ 食堂
20. ☐☐☐ renovate	20. ☐☐☐ 改装する

＊点線のところで折ると活動がしやすくなります。

Making Deals & Contracts

TOEIC Part 1 写真描写問題

LISTENING
Check Point!

言 い か え 表 現 に 気 を つ け よ う ②

　Part 1 では、写真の中に computer が写っていても、an electronic device や a laptop、an instrument などの言いかえ表現を用いて、そのアイテムを描写することがよくあります。同じ意味を表す別の表現が聞こえたら注意しましょう。

◆ Practice!

写真を参考にして、空所の語句を聞き取ってみましょう。

🎧 DL 109 ~ 110　◎ CD2-67　~　◎ CD2-68

1.

2.

1. Some glasses are ＿＿＿＿＿＿＿＿＿＿＿ ＿＿＿＿＿＿＿＿＿＿＿ liquid.

2. A man is using an ＿＿＿＿＿＿＿＿＿ for ＿＿＿＿＿＿＿＿＿.

◆ Try!

下の写真に関する英文が4つ読まれます。写真を最も適切に描写している選択肢を選びましょう。

↻ CheckLink　🎧 DL 111 ~ 112　◎ CD2-69　~　◎ CD2-70

1.

Ⓐ Ⓑ Ⓒ Ⓓ

2.

Ⓐ Ⓑ Ⓒ Ⓓ

TOEIC Part **4** 説明文問題

位 置 を 示 す 語 句 は 注 意 し て 聞 こ う

Part 4 では、位置を示す語句にも要注意です。right/left、front/back(rear)、behind などの位置を示す語と、その位置に関する情報（「何があるか」「誰がいるか」「何をしているか」など）を結びつけて理解するよう心がけましょう。

💎 Practice!

次の英文を聞き、（　　）に位置を表す語句を入れて、「どこで」「誰が」「何を」するのか考えてみましょう。　　🎧 DL 113 ~ 116　◎CD2-71 ~ ◎CD2-74

1. The man went into the bathroom at the (　　　　　　　　) of the room.

どこで _____　誰が _____　何をする _____

2. Register at the table on the (　　　　　　　　) side of the room.

どこで _____　誰が _____　何をする _____

3. The theater was so packed that some people were standing at the

(　　　　　　　).

どこで _____　誰が _____　何をする _____

4. The girl always sits at the (　　　　　　　) of the class.

どこで _____　誰が _____　何をする _____

💎 Try!

説明文を聞き、以下の設問に対して最も適切な答えを選択肢から選びましょう。

🔄CheckLink　🎧 DL 117 ~ 120　◎CD2-75 ~ ◎CD2-78

1. Who is this announcement intended for?

(A) Construction workers　　(B) Students

(C) Business people　　(D) Researchers　　　Ⓐ　Ⓑ　Ⓒ　Ⓓ

2. What is necessary to register for the event?

(A) A driving license　　(B) A picture ID card

(C) An invitation card　　(D) A member's card　　Ⓐ　Ⓑ　Ⓒ　Ⓓ

3. Where should people go if they want to discuss business?

(A) Go to the booth at the back

(B) Use a credit card and register

(C) Go to the booth at the front of the room

(D) Go to the registration table on the right side　　Ⓐ　Ⓑ　Ⓒ　Ⓓ

Improve Your TOEIC Listening Skills!

Part 4

TOEIC Part 4 形式の音声を聞き、以下の空所を埋めましょう。1回目は通常のスピードで、2回目はポーズ入りの音声が流れます。

※各空所はすべて正解した場合に、(﹏﹏﹏) は3点、(＿＿) は2点、(＿＿) は1点として採点します（部分点はありません）。

🎧 DL 121 ~ 122　◎ CD2-79 ~ ◎ CD2-80

MLJ Entertainment Park has (1.＿＿＿＿＿＿) a corporate marketing (2.﹏﹏﹏﹏﹏﹏﹏) with BNN Communications Corporation. (3.﹏﹏﹏﹏﹏﹏﹏﹏) co-sponsoring Rose Park Company, BNN Communications Corporation (4.＿＿＿＿＿) marketing activities (5.＿＿＿＿ ＿＿＿＿) advertisements and (6.﹏﹏﹏﹏﹏﹏) that (7.﹏﹏﹏﹏) enhance advertising effects. Rose Park Company provides a beautiful rose garden which (8.＿＿＿＿ ＿＿＿＿) the center of the MLJ Entertainment Park site. MLJ has a total of (9.＿＿＿＿) corporate marketing partner companies (10.＿＿＿＿＿) BNN Communications Corporation.

上の説明文に関する以下の設問に対して、最も適切な答えを選択肢から選びましょう。 ↻ CheckLink

1. What is the report mainly about?
- (A) A partnership contract between two companies
- (B) A recent customers' trend
- (C) A takeover of an online business
- (D) A history of the amusement park

Ⓐ Ⓑ Ⓒ Ⓓ

2. What is mentioned about Rose Park Company?
- (A) It targets young customers only.
- (B) It has expanded to Australia recently.
- (C) It provides a beautiful flower garden.
- (D) It is located near an amusement park.

Ⓐ Ⓑ Ⓒ Ⓓ

3. How many companies does MLJ Entertainment Park have a partnership with?
- (A) 15　(B) 20　(C) 25　(D) 30

Ⓐ Ⓑ Ⓒ Ⓓ

Dictation Score ／20

動 名 詞 と to 不 定 詞 の 違 い を お さ え よ う

　動詞の後ろには、動名詞がくる場合と to 不定詞がくる場合があります。また、動詞によっては、どちらか一方しか後ろにこない場合もあり、両方ともくる場合には、それぞれ意味が異なることがあります。なお、前置詞の後ろは、必ず動名詞の形（-ing）となります。

後ろに動名詞しかこない動詞

例　avoid, consider, deny, keep, mind, practice, quit

後ろに to 不定詞しかこない動詞

例　allow, decide, force, hesitate, persuade, plan, refuse

後ろに両方ともくるが意味が異なる動詞

例　forget, regret, remember

前置詞の後ろにくる動名詞

例　be accustomed to* -ing,　look forward to* -ing,　without -ing

(* to はここでは前置詞)

Practice!

[　　] 内から正しい語句を選び、文を完成させましょう。　　CheckLink

1. I am looking forward to [(A) hear / (B) hearing] from you.

2. Stop [(A) to include / (B) including] such dangerous clauses in the contract.

3. He is considering [(A) to make / (B) making] a contract with Yanaka Housing.

4. We decided not [(A) to work / (B) working] with the company.

Try!

空所に入る語句として最も適切な選択肢を選び、文を完成させましょう。　　CheckLink

1. Doing business without ------- any contract is really a bad practice.

　(A) having　　(B) have　　(C) to have　　(D) has had

Ⓐ　Ⓑ　Ⓒ　Ⓓ

2. The document says that none of the employees are allowed ------ during business hours.

(A) smoking   (B) to smoke   (C) have smoked   (D) smoke

Ⓐ Ⓑ Ⓒ Ⓓ

3. The company has stopped ------- employees, but it is still having trouble fixing the contract problems with several customers.

(A) laying off   (B) lay off   (C) to lay off   (D) have laid off

Ⓐ Ⓑ Ⓒ Ⓓ

4. As our warranty on the product says, we will send a technician to your home within one working day after ------- your call.

(A) reception   (B) receiving   (C) recipient   (D) received

Ⓐ Ⓑ Ⓒ Ⓓ

5. City workers have become accustomed ------- the rules set by the new mayor.

(A) to observe   (B) observe   (C) have observed   (D) to observing

Ⓐ Ⓑ Ⓒ Ⓓ

6. For a long time, he has denied ------- with his lawyer to talk about legal issues.

(A) meeting   (B) to meet   (C) to have met   (D) meet

Ⓐ Ⓑ Ⓒ Ⓓ

7. The company has managed to prevent itself from going bankrupt by ------- its terms of business with the customers.

(A) breached   (B) breach   (C) breaching   (D) to breach

Ⓐ Ⓑ Ⓒ Ⓓ

8. Do not forget ------- even the minute changes in the wordings of the contract.

(A) checking   (B) have checked   (C) check   (D) to check

Ⓐ Ⓑ Ⓒ Ⓓ

9. Would you mind ------- each clause of the document with me so that no further mistakes will be made?

(A) to review   (B) reviewing   (C) review   (D) to have reviewed

Ⓐ Ⓑ Ⓒ Ⓓ

10. The company's newly introduced insurance policy is worth ------- even for the younger generation.

(A) consider   (B) to consider   (C) considered   (D) considering

Ⓐ Ⓑ Ⓒ Ⓓ

設 問 の 順 番 を 利 用 し て 情 報 を 探 そ う

　Part 7 では、文書で述べられている順番に設問が作られる傾向があります。このルールを知っていると、2問目の答えの根拠となる箇所は、1問目の答えの根拠となる場所よりも後に出てくるということが予想できます。

◆ **Practice!**

次の文書を読み、以下の設問の答えがある箇所を○で囲みましょう。

1. When was this bill issued for Mr. Thomas?

2. How did Mr. Thomas pay for his membership renewal?

3. When was the renewal date of Mr. Thomas's membership?

4. How much did Mr. Thomas pay?

British Community Sports Center
Membership Renewal Notice

Mr. Philip Thomas
6-20 Queen Avenue
London

Bill date: May 30, 2021

Your membership is going to expire on June 30. Please detach and return the form below with your check (or credit card receipt) by then, using the enclosed return envelope. We recommend that you take advantage of the 20 percent discount by upgrading your membership status to two-year membership.

-------------------------------- Cut here --------------------------------

Payment Information
[　×　] Credit card receipt enclosed
[　　　] Check enclosed
Card #: e014-1892-1442-451b
Name on Card: Philip Thomas
ID on Card: IT-K105
Renewal Date: June 5, 2021
Frequency of use (per month): 20

Please check the appropriate box.
[　×　] £80 Two-year Membership Fee / Year
[　　　] £100 One-year Membership Fee
Enclosed is the (~~check~~ / credit card receipt) of £160

Signature: *Philip Thomas*
Date: *June 2, 2021*

Try!

左の文書に関する以下の設問に対して、最も適切な答えを選択肢から選びましょう。 CheckLink

1. What is Mr. Thomas encouraged to do?

(A) Sign up to the event

(B) Buy products online

(C) Visit the sports gym

(D) Renew his membership

Ⓐ　Ⓑ　Ⓒ　Ⓓ

2. How can Mr. Thomas get a discount?

(A) By returning the envelope by June 5

(B) By upgrading his membership status to two years

(C) By paying check earlier than June 5

(D) By introducing someone to the sports center

Ⓐ　Ⓑ　Ⓒ　Ⓓ

3. What is implied about Mr. Thomas?

(A) He is going to leave the town soon.

(B) He has a diving license.

(C) He often visits the sports center.

(D) He works for a famous IT company.

Ⓐ　Ⓑ　Ⓒ　Ⓓ

Review! Unit 10

☐ Part 1 では、同じ意味を表す (1.　　　　　) が聞こえたら注意。

☐ Part 4 では、(2.　　　　) を示す語句に注意して聞く。

☐ (3.　　　　)、(4.　　　　)、(5.　　　　) などは後ろに動名詞しかこない。
allow、decide、refuse などは後ろに (6.　　　　) しかこない。

☐ forget to ... は「(7.　　　　　　)」の意味になり、forget -ing は
「(8.　　　　　)」の意味になる。

☐ look forward to ... の後ろは (9.　　　　) がくる。

☐ Part 7 では、文書で述べられている (10.　　　　) に設問が作られる傾向がある。

Build Up Your TOEIC Vocabulary!

Making Deals & Contracts

単語を覚えて、30秒以内にいくつ言えるか、ペアで確認してみましょう。

手順

① 英単語を見て意味を言う役とチェックする役に分かれて、お互いの教科書を交換する。
② 英単語を見て意味を言う役は、日本語訳を筆箱などで隠す。
③ 教員の合図とともに、1～20の英単語を見て意味を言う（わからない場合は Let me skip it! と相手に伝えましょう）。
④ チェック役は相手の答えを聞き、正解していたら日本語訳の □ ボックスに左端から✓を入れる。
⑤ 同じ手順を日本語訳→英単語でも行う。

DL 123　　CD2-81

1.	terms and conditions	1. 契約条件
2.	insurance policy	2. 保険契約（証書）
3.	valid	3. 有効な、効力がある
4.	expire	4. 期限が切れる
5.	agreement	5. 同意
6.	party	6. （契約の）当事者
7.	violation	7. 違反
8.	cancel	8. 取り消す
9.	lease	9. 賃貸借契約
10.	clause	10. 条項
11.	negotiate	11. 交渉する
12.	draft	12. 草案
13.	deal	13. 商取引、売買
14.	sign	14. 署名する
15.	signature	15. 署名
16.	conclude	16. （契約を）結ぶ
17.	legally binding	17. 法的拘束力がある
18.	damage	18. 損害
19.	compensation	19. 賠償
20.	acceptance	20. （契約の）承諾

＊点線のところで折ると活動がしやすくなります。

Public Service

TOEIC Part 1　写真描写問題

効 率 的 な 選 択 肢 の 幅 の 狭 め 方 を 学 ぼ う

　Part 1 で読み上げられる 4 つの選択肢には、写真の中で描写されていない人や物を含むことがあります。その場合、正解ではない選択肢である可能性が高いので、注意しながら聞きましょう。

◆ Practice!

写真を参考にして、空所の語句を聞き取ってみましょう。

🎧 DL 124 ~ 125　　◉ CD3-02　~　◉ CD3-03

1.

2.

1. A man is _____ _____ _____.

2. People are sitting _____ _____ _____.

◆ Try!

下の写真に関する英文が 4 つ読まれます。写真を最も適切に描写している選択肢を選びましょう。

⟳ CheckLink　🎧 DL 126 ~ 127　　◉ CD3-04　~　◉ CD3-05

1.

Ⓐ　Ⓑ　Ⓒ　Ⓓ

2.

Ⓐ　Ⓑ　Ⓒ　Ⓓ

TOEIC Part 2 応答問題

付 加 疑 問 文 に 強 く な ろ う

　付加疑問文とは、文末に aren't you (are you) ？や didn't you (did you) ？のような否定形（あるいは肯定形）がつき、「…ですよね」という同意を求める文のことです。この疑問文への正しい答えを見つけるためには、文末（後半）の否定形（あるいは肯定形）に惑わされることなく、前半の内容に対してのみ Yes/No で応答するようにしましょう。

以下の付加疑問文に対する正しい答えを選択肢から選びましょう。　　　　CheckLink

1. Berlin is the capital of Germany, isn't it?

[(A) Yes, it is. / (B) No, it isn't.]

2. It is four people who wrote this textbook*, isn't it?

[(A) Yes, it is. / (B) No, it isn't.]

3. This textbook is for preparation for the TOEIC L&R test, isn't it?

[(A) Yes, it is. / (B) No, it isn't.]

4. The publisher of this textbook* is not KINSEIDO, is it?

[(A) Yes, it is. / (B) No, it isn't.]

*this textbook は皆さんの使っているこの教科書のことと考えてみましょう。

Try!

質問文を聞き、最も適切な答えを選択肢から選びましょう。

CheckLink　　DL 128 ~ 132　　CD3-06　~　CD3-10

1. Mark your answer on your answer sheet.　　Ⓐ　Ⓑ　Ⓒ

2. Mark your answer on your answer sheet.　　Ⓐ　Ⓑ　Ⓒ

3. Mark your answer on your answer sheet.　　Ⓐ　Ⓑ　Ⓒ

4. Mark your answer on your answer sheet.　　Ⓐ　Ⓑ　Ⓒ

5. Mark your answer on your answer sheet.　　Ⓐ　Ⓑ　Ⓒ

Improve Your TOEIC Listening Skills!

Part **1** & Part **2**

TOEIC Part 1 および Part 2 形式の音声を聞き、以下の空所を埋めましょう。1回目は通常のスピードで、2回目はポーズ入りの音声が流れます。その後、1に関しては写真を最もよく描写しているものを、2および3に関しては質問文に対する最も適切な答えを選択肢から選びましょう。

※各空所はすべて正解した場合に、(～～～) は3点、(＿＿＿) は2点、(＿＿＿) は1点として採点します（部分点はありません）。

1.

CheckLink 🎧 DL 133 ~ 134　◎ CD3-11 ~ ◎ CD3-12

(A) A boy is (¹.＿＿＿＿＿ ＿＿＿＿＿) the slide.

(B) A boy is climbing (².＿＿＿＿＿ ＿＿＿＿＿).

(C) They are (³.＿＿＿＿＿ ＿＿＿＿＿) caps.

(D) The boys are playing (⁴.＿＿＿＿＿ ＿＿＿＿＿ ＿＿＿＿＿).

Ⓐ Ⓑ Ⓒ Ⓓ

CheckLink 🎧 DL 135 ~ 136　◎ CD3-13 ~ ◎ CD3-14

2. (¹.～～～～～～～～～～～～～～～～～～～) the proposal for the (².＿＿＿＿＿) city concert?

(A) (³.＿＿＿＿＿, ＿＿＿＿＿ ＿＿＿＿＿).

(B) It's (⁴.＿＿＿＿＿ ＿＿＿＿＿ ＿＿＿＿＿).

(C) I would like to (⁵.＿＿＿＿＿) that proposal.

Ⓐ Ⓑ Ⓒ

CheckLink 🎧 DL 137 ~ 138　◎ CD3-15 ~ ◎ CD3-16

3. (¹.＿＿＿＿＿ ＿＿＿＿＿) does the city hall (².＿＿＿＿＿)?

(A) They are (³.＿＿＿＿＿) the city hall.

(B) (⁴.＿＿＿＿＿) p.m.

(C) Yes, I've (⁵.＿＿＿＿＿ ＿＿＿＿＿ ＿＿＿＿＿).

Ⓐ Ⓑ Ⓒ

Dictation Score ／20

時 や 理 由 、 譲 歩 を 表 す 接 続 詞 に 注 意 し よ う

　接続詞には文をつなぎ合わせる働きがあります。and、but、or を使って 2 つの文を対等に並べる場合と、接続詞で導かれた部分が時や理由、譲歩などを表す場合とがあります。

文を対等に並べる接続詞

　　and（…も）、but（しかし）、or（または）

時や理由、譲歩などを表す接続詞

　　when（…のときに）、while（…する間に）、because（…なので）、although/
　　though（…ではあるが）、if（もし…ならば）、that（…ということ）

Practice!

[　　] 内から正しい語句を選び、文を完成させましょう。　　CheckLink

1. Please call me [(A) if / (B) though] you have a question.

2. He watched TV [(A) because / (B) though] he had an exam the next day.

3. I didn't know [(A) while / (B) that] the store was closed on that day.

4. The office entrance was locked [(A) when / (B) that] she came early in the morning.

Try!

空所に入る語句として最も適切な選択肢を選び、文を完成させましょう。　　CheckLink

1. Please use public transportation ------- you come to the concert hall.
(A) though　　(B) nor　　(C) that　　(D) when

Ⓐ　Ⓑ　Ⓒ　Ⓓ

2. We were late for school ------- the train service was delayed for more than half an hour.
(A) nor　　(B) but　　(C) because　　(D) although

Ⓐ　Ⓑ　Ⓒ　Ⓓ

3. ------- the garbage is not separated properly, the collector won't pick it up.
(A) But　　(B) That　　(C) And　　(D) If

Ⓐ　Ⓑ　Ⓒ　Ⓓ

4. ------- the train stopped suddenly in the accident, no passengers were killed or injured.

(A) If   (B) Although   (C) On   (D) At

Ⓐ Ⓑ Ⓒ Ⓓ

5. Power outages are rather rare these days, ------- it is always a good thing to be prepared.

(A) for   (B) nor   (C) but   (D) that

Ⓐ Ⓑ Ⓒ Ⓓ

6. Public transportation is economical ------- also it is environmentally friendly.

(A) and   (B) nor   (C) or   (D) but

Ⓐ Ⓑ Ⓒ Ⓓ

7. She makes it a rule to read a book ------- she is on the train.

(A) though   (B) nor   (C) while   (D) that

Ⓐ Ⓑ Ⓒ Ⓓ

8. We were at a loss ------- electric power suddenly went off last night.

(A) but   (B) or   (C) nor   (D) when

Ⓐ Ⓑ Ⓒ Ⓓ

9. The bus service is cancelled today ------- there is a thick layer of snow on the roads.

(A) because   (B) and   (C) or   (D) but

Ⓐ Ⓑ Ⓒ Ⓓ

10. The notice says ------- the bus fare will be raised by five percent from next month.

(A) when   (B) while   (C) that   (D) though

Ⓐ Ⓑ Ⓒ Ⓓ

告 知 文 （ Notice ） で は ポ イ ン ト を お さ え よ う

　告知文を読む際にはおさえるべきポイントが3つあります。それは、
① 「誰が」その告知文を発行・掲載しているのか
② 「誰に向けて」のメッセージなのか
③ 「何を」告知しているのか
ということです。これらの3つをおさえて、しっかりと情報を読み取りましょう。もし明確に情報が書かれていない場合でも、文脈から情報を推測することが大切です。

Practice!

次の3つの文書から、告知文について以下の情報を読み取って、英語または日本語で書き入れましょう。

「誰が」：_____

「誰に向けて」：_____

「何を」：_____

Notice

KIU management will be upgrading the water metering system. During the upgrading exercise, there will be water disruption. Please check the water disruption from the time schedule chart below.

PLACE	DATE	TIME
Room 101~105	October 9th	11 a.m. ~ 1 p.m.
Room 201~205	October 9th	2 p.m. ~ 5 p.m.
Room 301~305	October 10th	11 a.m. ~ 1 p.m.

We apologize in advance for any inconvenience caused.

For information call: 89-9971-6723

To:	Sarah Baily <sara-hsarad@kiumanagement.com>
From:	Ted Hamilton <tatoted@kiumanagement.com>
Subject:	the draft of the notice
Date:	August 7

Hi, Sarah,

I have attached a draft of the notice that we're emailing to all residents of the apartment. We need to finalize the information on the notice by the day after tomorrow so that we can send it out by the weekend. Also, I'd like you to contact the water supplier to confirm the date and time of the upgrading exercise just in case.

Best wishes,

Ted

To:	Ted Hamilton <tatoted@kiumanagement.com>
From:	Sarah Baily <sara-hsarad@kiumanagement.com>
Subject:	Re: the draft of the notice
Date:	August 7

Hi, Ted,

Thank you for the draft. I checked it and found a couple of mistakes that must be corrected. In the last line, the phone number ends in a six, not three. Also, I called Megan, the manager of the water supplier company, and she said the exercise on the 10th starts from 12 o'clock. I know you have a meeting this afternoon, so I could take care of these mistakes for you.

Best,

Sarah

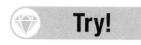

Try!

前ページの３つの文書に関する以下の設問に対して、最も適切な答えを選択肢から選びましょう。

1. What is the purpose of the notice?

(A) To ask the residents to check the water metering system

(B) To show the residents the renovation plan

(C) To tell the residents to get ready for evacuation

(D) To inform the residents to prepare for water disruption

Ⓐ　Ⓑ　Ⓒ　Ⓓ

2. Where does Mr. Hamilton most likely work?

(A) At the hotel

(B) At the building management company

(C) At the water supplier company

(D) At the real estate agency

Ⓐ　Ⓑ　Ⓒ　Ⓓ

3. By when does Mr. Hamilton want to finalize the notice?

(A) By tomorrow

(B) By this afternoon

(C) By August 9

(D) By the weekend

Ⓐ　Ⓑ　Ⓒ　Ⓓ

4. What did Mr. Hamilton ask Ms. Baily to do?

(A) Contact the water supplier company

(B) Email the residents

(C) Place the order

(D) Set up the meeting

Ⓐ　Ⓑ　Ⓒ　Ⓓ

5. According to the second e-mail, what will Mr. Hamilton most likely do?

(A) He will visit a water supplier.

(B) He will meet a client.

(C) He will do some exercise.

(D) He will attend a meeting.

Ⓐ　Ⓑ　Ⓒ　Ⓓ

108

Unit 11

☐ Part 1 では、(¹.   ) 人や物を含む選択肢は間違いの場合
が多い。

☐ (².   ) とは、文末に (³.   ) の
ような否定形（あるいは肯定形）がつき、(⁴.   ) という
同意を求める意味を持つ文のこと。答えるときは、(⁵.   )
の否定形（あるいは肯定形）に惑わされることなく、(⁶.   )
に対してのみ Yes/No で応答するとよい。

☐ 接続詞は (⁷.   ) をつなぐ役割を果たす。

☐ 告知文では、「(⁸.   )」「(⁹.   )」、
そして「(¹⁰.   )」告知しているのかに注目する。

Build Up Your TOEIC Vocabulary!

Public Service

単語を覚えて、30秒以内にいくつ言えるか、ペアで確認してみましょう。

手順

① 英単語を見て意味を言う役とチェックする役に分かれて、お互いの教科書を交換する。

② 英単語を見て意味を言う役は、日本語訳を筆箱などで隠す。

③ 教員の合図とともに、1〜20の英単語を見て意味を言う（わからない場合は Let me skip it! と相手に伝えましょう）。

④ チェック役は相手の答えを聞き、正解していたら日本語訳の □ ボックスに左端から✓を入れる。

⑤ 同じ手順を日本語訳→英単語でも行う。

DL 139　CD3-17

1.	vehicle	1. 乗り物
2.	fare	2. 運賃
3.	traffic	3. 交通（量）
4.	subway	4. 地下鉄
5.	reform	5. 改革
6.	commute	6. 通勤（通学）する
7.	public transportation	7. 公共交通機関
8.	traffic jam	8. 交通渋滞
9.	be delayed	9. 遅延して
10.	be cancelled	10. 運休して
11.	passenger	11. 乗客
12.	mayor	12. 市長
13.	city council	13. 市議会
14.	electric power	14. 電力
15.	power outage	15. 停電
16.	water supply	16. 上水道
17.	fire station	17. 消防署
18.	garbage collection	18. ゴミ収集
19.	ongoing	19. 進行中の
20.	governor	20. 知事

＊点線のところで折ると活動がしやすくなります。

TOEIC Part 1 写真描写問題

LISTENING Check Point!

物 が 主 語 に な る 場 合 に 注 意 し よ う

Part 1 では、人だけでなく物が主語として使われることが多くあります。物が主語の場合、受け身の表現が使われることが多いので、それをヒントに示されている状態を聞き取りましょう。

例 Some files **have been piled** up on the desk.
（いくつかのファイルがデスクの上に積み重ねられてあります）

The ladder **is being leaned** against the wall.
（はしごが壁に立て掛けられているところです）

Practice!

写真を参考にして、空所の語句を聞き取ってみましょう。

🎧 DL 140 ~ 141 　◎ CD3-18 ~ ◎ CD3-19

1. 　　**2.**

1. The credit card _____ _____ into the ATM.

2. Some screens _____ _____ _____ in front of the man.

Try!

下の写真に関する英文が 4 つ読まれます。写真を最も適切に描写している選択肢を選びましょう。

⟳CheckLink 　🎧 DL 142 ~ 143 　◎ CD3-20 ~ ◎ CD3-21

1. 　　**2.**

Ⓐ Ⓑ Ⓒ Ⓓ 　　　　　　Ⓐ Ⓑ Ⓒ Ⓓ

LISTENING
Check Point!

設問を先読みして聞き取りのポイントをしぼろう ②

Part 3 では、比較的長い会話文が読み上げられますので、音声が始まる前に設問（できれば選択肢も）に目を通しておき、キーワードを頭の中に入れておきましょう。例えば、What is the man asked to do in the morning session? という設問であれば、「男性」「頼まれる内容」「朝のミーティングで」というように、聞き取るポイントをしぼっておくと、後のリスニングがしやすくなるでしょう。

Practice!

次の文を読み、どの部分にポイントをしぼればよいのかキーワードを書いてみましょう。

1. What time will the store open tomorrow?　　　　[　　　　　　　　　]
2. How long will the workshop last?　　　　　　　[　　　　　　　　　]
3. What should Mr. Hoffman do if he has a question?　[　　　　　　　　　]

Try!

会話を聞き、以下の設問に対して最も適切な答えを選択肢から選びましょう。

⟲CheckLink　🎧 DL 144 ~ 147　◎ CD3-22　~　◎ CD3-25

1. What is the topic of the conversation?
　(A) The morning news
　(B) Recruitment
　(C) Annual meeting
　(D) Business conditions

Ⓐ Ⓑ Ⓒ Ⓓ

2. What was different from the last meeting?
　(A) The numbers
　(B) The chart
　(C) The table
　(D) The instruction

Ⓐ Ⓑ Ⓒ Ⓓ

3. Why are Simon and Sheryl going to meet the manager?
　(A) To finalize the data
　(B) To introduce the staff
　(C) To get his approval
　(D) To correct the date

Ⓐ Ⓑ Ⓒ Ⓓ

Improve Your TOEIC Listening Skills!

Part **3**

TOEIC Part 3 形式の音声を聞き、以下の空所を埋めましょう。1回目は通常のスピードで、2回目はポーズ入りの音声が流れます。

※各空所はすべて正解した場合に、(～～～) は3点、(＿＿) は2点、(＿＿) は1点として採点します（部分点はありません）。

🎧 DL 148 ~ 149   ◎ CD3-26 ~ ◎ CD3-27

W: I deposited $500 into my (¹.＿＿＿＿＿＿＿＿＿＿＿＿), but when I tried to (².＿＿＿＿＿＿＿＿＿＿), the (³.＿＿＿＿＿＿) outside wouldn't let me (⁴＿＿＿＿＿＿＿＿＿＿＿).

M: I see. When did you make the (⁵.＿＿＿＿＿＿)?

W: On Friday. Do you need the transaction (⁶.＿＿＿＿＿＿＿)?

M: No, thank you. If you deposited it on Friday, the funds will be (⁷.＿＿＿＿＿＿) to you this afternoon. We (⁸.＿＿＿＿＿＿＿) all deposits for at least (⁹.＿＿＿＿＿＿＿＿＿＿＿) to protect (¹⁰.＿＿＿＿＿＿) clients and the bank from fraud.

上の会話に関する以下の設問に対して、最も適切な答えを選択肢から選びましょう。 ↻ CheckLink

1. Where does the conversation most likely take place?
   (A) At a supermarket   (B) At a bank
   (C) At a retail shop   (D) At a travel agency   Ⓐ Ⓑ Ⓒ Ⓓ

2. What information does the woman try to give the man?
   (A) Her account number   (B) Her home address
   (C) Her security code   (D) Her transaction code   Ⓐ Ⓑ Ⓒ Ⓓ

3. When can the woman withdraw her deposit?
   (A) Monday   (B) Tuesday
   (C) Wednesday   (D) Thursday   Ⓐ Ⓑ Ⓒ Ⓓ

Dictation Score ╱ **20**

副詞と形容詞の違いをおさえよう

副詞は動詞や形容詞、文全体を修飾しますが、名詞を修飾することはできません。これに対して、形容詞は名詞を修飾し、補語になることもできますが、動詞や形容詞、文全体を修飾することはできません。

TOEIC 頻出の副詞

 absolutely, actually, approximately, consequently, eventually,

frequently, hardly, rarely, scarcely, substantially, surprisingly

Practice!

[　] 内から正しい語句を選び、文を完成させましょう。　　　CheckLink

1. I could [(A) hard / (B) hardly] follow the financial news on TV.

2. Going out to dinner with colleagues is [(A) rare / (B) rarely].

3. Give us some [(A) additional / (B) additionally] information about the investment, please.

4. The CFO has been very [(A) busy / (B) busily] ever since the stock listing of his company.

Try!

空所に入る語句として最も適切な選択肢を選び、文を完成させましょう。　　CheckLink

1. It is believed that the company has a huge deficit, although detailed data are -------.

(A) rare　　(B) scarce　　(C) scarcely　　(D) hard

Ⓐ　Ⓑ　Ⓒ　Ⓓ

2. The CEO spoke to us ------- before moving off to another business meeting.

(A) brief　　(B) briefly　　(C) briefer　　(D) brevity

Ⓐ　Ⓑ　Ⓒ　Ⓓ

3. -------, money transfers to the company were suddenly halted.

(A) Surprised　　(B) Surprising　　(C) Surprisingly　　(D) Surprise

Ⓐ　Ⓑ　Ⓒ　Ⓓ

4. A ------- raise in salary is hardly expected nowadays.

(A) substantial   (B) substantially   (C) substance   (D) substantiated

Ⓐ Ⓑ Ⓒ Ⓓ

5. The executive board objected ------- to some of the conditions offered by the M & A company.

(A) strong   (B) strongly   (C) strength   (D) strongest

Ⓐ Ⓑ Ⓒ Ⓓ

6. Her investment advice ------- combines a long-term perspective with a short-term one.

(A) skillfully   (B) skillful   (C) skilled   (D) skills

Ⓐ Ⓑ Ⓒ Ⓓ

7. After ------- failure to gain consumer support, Keyton's new spreadsheet program has been withdrawn from the market.

(A) repeatedly   (B) repeated   (C) repeat   (D) repeats

Ⓐ Ⓑ Ⓒ Ⓓ

8. When sending money to foreign countries, using the remittance service is -------.

(A) preferably   (B) preferable   (C) preferences   (D) prefer

Ⓐ Ⓑ Ⓒ Ⓓ

9. We have ------- three hundred inactive bank accounts at this branch alone.

(A) approximately   (B) approximate

(C) appropriate   (D) appropriately

Ⓐ Ⓑ Ⓒ Ⓓ

10. Bank transfer fraud has been a ------- topic in newspapers lately.

(A) frequently   (B) frequent   (C) tentativeness   (D) tentatively

Ⓐ Ⓑ Ⓒ Ⓓ

言 い か え 表 現 に 注 意 し よ う

以前、TOEIC の Part 1 では「言いかえ表現」が使われることに触れましたが（Unit 8 および 10 参照）、Part 7 でも、パッセージに書かれている表現が、設問中の選択肢で言いかえられていることがあります。例として、様々な台所用品が kitchen utensils あるいは kitchen tools と言いかえられることがあげられます。

Practice!

以下の表現は次の文書のどの表現の言いかえでしょうか。該当する部分に番号を付けて下線を引きましょう。

1. kitchen tools
2. projects
3. looking for
4. people

Starting a Franchise in Our Business

Founded nearly ten years ago, BLOD company has quickly grown to be a prominent retailer of quality kitchen accessories and items in the northeast of the country. We were recently described by industry journal *Modern Kitchen* as "Innovative retailer of the year," and last year won the *MUB Kitchen Award*. Starting later this year, we are expanding operations across the country. As a result, we are seeking a number of motivated, ambitious individuals to start franchises in our business. Interested individuals must have $150,000 or more capital, and should contact Michael Spry at 598-1089-0046 for further details.

Try!

左の文書に関する以下の設問に対して、最も適切な答えを選択肢から選びましょう。　⟲CheckLink

1. What is the purpose of this notice?

(A) To advertise the company

(B) To give an overview of the forthcoming event

(C) To encourage retailers to sell more goods

(D) To offer a business opportunity

Ⓐ　Ⓑ　Ⓒ　Ⓓ

2. What is inferred about BLOD company?

(A) It has a 20-year history.

(B) It provides excellent kitchen items.

(C) It has many overseas branches.

(D) It got unfavorable customers' feedback.

Ⓐ　Ⓑ　Ⓒ　Ⓓ

3. What criterion must the applicants meet?

(A) Franchises experience in the same field

(B) MUB Kitchen Awards

(C) A certain amount of capital

(D) Knowledge about kitchen tools

Ⓐ　Ⓑ　Ⓒ　Ⓓ

Review!　Unit 12

☐ Part 1 では、(1.　　　　　　　　　) が主語として使われることが多くある。

☐ Part 3 では、(2.　　　　　　　　) 会話文が読み上げられる。この場合、音声が始まる前に (3.　　　　　　　　) に目を通しておき、キーワードを頭の中に入れておくとよい。

☐ 副詞は (4.　　　　　　　　) および文全体を修飾できるが、
(5.　　　　　　　　) を修飾することはできない。形容詞は
(6.　　　　　　　　) を修飾し、(7.　　　　　　　　) にもなるが、
(8.　　　　　　　　) や形容詞、(9.　　　　　　　　) を修飾することはできない。

☐ Part 7 では、(10.　　　　　　　　) が、設問中の選択肢で言いかえられていることがある。

Build Up Your TOEIC Vocabulary!
Banking & Finance

単語を覚えて、30秒以内にいくつ言えるか、ペアで確認してみましょう。

手順

① 英単語を見て意味を言う役とチェックする役に分かれて、お互いの教科書を交換する。
② 英単語を見て意味を言う役は、日本語訳を筆箱などで隠す。
③ 教員の合図とともに、1〜20の英単語を見て意味を言う（わからない場合は Let me skip it! と相手に伝えましょう）。
④ チェック役は相手の答えを聞き、正解していたら日本語訳の □ ボックスに左端から✓を入れる。
⑤ 同じ手順を日本語訳→英単語でも行う。

🎧 DL 150　　💿 CD3-28

1. ☐☐☐ investment	1. ☐☐☐ 投資
2. ☐☐☐ deficit	2. ☐☐☐ 損失、赤字
3. ☐☐☐ deposit	3. ☐☐☐ 預金する、預金
4. ☐☐☐ withdraw	4. ☐☐☐ （預金を）引き出す
5. ☐☐☐ bank account	5. ☐☐☐ 銀行口座
6. ☐☐☐ fund	6. ☐☐☐ 資金
7. ☐☐☐ profit	7. ☐☐☐ 利益
8. ☐☐☐ debt	8. ☐☐☐ 借金、負債
9. ☐☐☐ stock price	9. ☐☐☐ 株価
10. ☐☐☐ financial institution	10. ☐☐☐ 金融機関
11. ☐☐☐ stock market	11. ☐☐☐ 株式市場
12. ☐☐☐ savings account	12. ☐☐☐ 普通預金口座
13. ☐☐☐ checking account	13. ☐☐☐ 当座預金口座
14. ☐☐☐ remittance	14. ☐☐☐ 送金
15. ☐☐☐ transfer	15. ☐☐☐ 振込
16. ☐☐☐ check	16. ☐☐☐ 小切手
17. ☐☐☐ money order	17. ☐☐☐ 郵便為替
18. ☐☐☐ interest rate	18. ☐☐☐ 利率
19. ☐☐☐ balance	19. ☐☐☐ 預金残高
20. ☐☐☐ PIN	20. ☐☐☐ 暗証番号

＊点線のところで折ると活動がしやすくなります。

TOEIC Part 1 　写真描写問題

選択肢の表現に注意しよう

　Part 1 における写真描写問題は、写真が撮られた「瞬間」のことを尋ねています。そこで、進行形（be -ing）で描写されることが多くなります。また、be about to ...（…しようとしている）や be going to ... / will（…するだろう）といった「これから起こること」を表す表現を含む選択肢は、誤りとなる可能性が高くなります。

Practice!

写真を参考にして、空所の語句を聞き取ってみましょう。その後、各文の内容が正しければ T（True）を、正しくなければ F（False）を選びましょう。

 DL 151 ~ 152　　◎ CD3-29　~　◎ CD3-30

1.

2.

1. Some people _____ _____ _____ presentations.　【T / F】

2. The lecturer _____ _____ _____ _____.　【T / F】

Try!

下の写真に関する英文が 4 つ読まれます。写真を最も適切に描写している選択肢を選びましょう。

CheckLink DL 153 ~ 154　　◎ CD3-31　~　◎ CD3-32

1.

Ⓐ　Ⓑ　Ⓒ　Ⓓ

2.

Ⓐ　Ⓑ　Ⓒ　Ⓓ

TOEIC Part 4 説明文問題

流 れ を つ か ん で 聞 こ う

Part 4 の説明文では多くの場合、「目的（概要）」→「詳細の説明」→「次の行動の指示」という決まった流れがあります。その流れを意識しながら聞いてみましょう。

以下の 4 つの文が自然な流れになるよう、[　] に番号を入れましょう。

1. Our purpose is to share with you the skills and techniques for better consumer counseling.

2. Thank you for coming to this seminar.

3. Excellent speakers will give us talks regarding these topics.

4. Those who are interested in the first speaker, please go to Room A.

[　　] → [　　] → [　　] → [　　]

説明文を聞き、以下の設問に対して最も適切な答えを選択肢から選びましょう。

CheckLink 　 DL 155 ~ 158 　 CD3-33 ～ CD3-36

Global Marketing Seminars	
Room 301	Celina Hunter "Inbound marketing strategy"
Room 302	Joyce Ford "Digital marketing strategy"
Room 303	Julia Cotsworth "Customer-first strategy"
Room 304	Daisy Johnson "Influencer Marketing strategy"

1. Look at the graphic. Who is the speaker?

(A) Celina Hunter 　　　　　　　　(B) Joyce Ford

(C) Julia Cotsworth 　　　　　　　(D) Daisy Johnson

Ⓐ Ⓑ Ⓒ Ⓓ

2. What does the speaker prefer to do at the end of the seminar?

(A) Have a discussion with the audience 　(B) Have a break

(C) Invite questions 　　　　　　　(D) Do some group work

Ⓐ Ⓑ Ⓒ Ⓓ

3. Where do the participants find the URL for the seminar?

(A) On the handout 　　　　　　　(B) On the information board

(C) On the brochure 　　　　　　　(D) On the presentation slides

Ⓐ Ⓑ Ⓒ Ⓓ

Improve Your TOEIC Listening Skills!

Part **4**

TOEIC Part 4 形式の音声を聞き、以下の空所を埋めましょう。1回目は通常のスピードで、2回目はポーズ入りの音声が流れます。

※各空所はすべて正解した場合に、（﹏﹏）は3点、（＿＿）は2点、（＿＿）は1点として採点します（部分点はありません）。

🎧 DL 159 ~ 160　◎ CD3-37　~　◎ CD3-38

Good morning everyone and thank you for coming to this (¹._____).
Today, you'll learn about (².﹏﹏﹏﹏﹏﹏﹏﹏﹏﹏
﹏﹏﹏). Our instructor this morning, Joseph Morgan, will talk about
aggressive (³.﹏﹏﹏﹏﹏﹏﹏﹏). Meanwhile, Bob Tracer will be
speaking to you about (⁴._____ _____ _____) a successful
trading plan (⁵.﹏﹏﹏﹏﹏﹏﹏﹏﹏﹏). After the seminar,
each of you will have the (⁶._____) for some (⁷.﹏﹏﹏﹏
﹏﹏﹏) with trading software in the computer lab. We'd like you all to
take the time after the seminar today to (⁸._____ _____) a
questionnaire. If you have questions, please (⁹._____ _____
_____) ask our support staff member, George Brown, at any time.

上の説明文に関する以下の設問に対して、最も適切な答えを選択肢から選びましょう。

↻ CheckLink

1. Who will talk about a successful trading plan?
   (A) The speaker
   (B) Joseph Morgan
   (C) Bob Tracer
   (D) George Brown
   Ⓐ Ⓑ Ⓒ Ⓓ

2. What will the participants do after the seminar?
   (A) View a brief demonstration
   (B) Learn how to create the software
   (C) Experience the software directly
   (D) Submit the marketing plan
   Ⓐ Ⓑ Ⓒ Ⓓ

3. Who is George Brown?
   (A) A software developer
   (B) A language instructor
   (C) A graphic designer
   (D) A support staff member
   Ⓐ Ⓑ Ⓒ Ⓓ

Dictation Score	/20

文 脈 を と ら え よ う

Part 6 では、文脈をとらえていないと正解を選べない問題がよく出題されます。空所の前後を見るだけではなく、全体の話の流れをおさえながら、正しい選択肢を選びましょう。

 **Practice!**

以下はセミナーの申し込みに関する文章です。よく読んで、文脈に合っていない文を二重線で消しましょう。

◆ How can we apply for the seminar?

First of all, please fill in the blanks on the application form. The presenter is Mr. Yamada, who is a well-known scholar. The seminar fee is $400. It should be paid either by credit card or by check. He needs to have a bank account. The seminar will start on Monday. If you have any questions, please send an email.

次の文を読んで、空所に入る最も適切な選択肢を選びましょう。　　　　　Ｃ CheckLink

How to Apply

Admissions deadline: September 3

Applicants should complete and submit the online application form to Active Presentation and upload all required supplemental documents ------- **1.** September 3.

------- **2.** manuscripts should be mailed directly to the coordinator during the period from July 2 to September 3.

------- **3.** Decisions on admissions and financial aid awards are made in November or early December for the ------- **4.**.

---

1. (A) on
  (B) in
  (C) at
  (D) by

　　　　　　　　　　　　　　Ⓐ　Ⓑ　Ⓒ　Ⓓ

2. (A) Printed
  (B) Printing
  (C) Printable
  (D) Printer

　　　　　　　　　　　　　　Ⓐ　Ⓑ　Ⓒ　Ⓓ

3. (A) Applicants are only accepted for entry to the spring semester.
  (B) The online application system was introduced last year.
  (C) You need to register on our site to set up email alerts.
  (D) Your supplemental documents provide additional information.

　　　　　　　　　　　　　　Ⓐ　Ⓑ　Ⓒ　Ⓓ

4. (A) two years
  (B) following year
  (C) three years ago
  (D) last year

　　　　　　　　　　　　　　Ⓐ　Ⓑ　Ⓒ　Ⓓ

メ ー ル 内 で 使 わ れ る 語 句 を お さ え よ う

Part 7 では、メール形式の文書がよく出題されます。メールでは独特の表現（p.s.「追伸」、attachment「添付資料」など）が使われることがありますので、よく使われる語句を整理して覚えておきましょう。

◈ Practice!

以下の語に相当する日本語訳を選択肢から選びましょう。

C CheckLink

1. subject [   ]   **2.** reply [   ]   **3.** inquiry [   ]
4. attached [   ]   **5.** enclosed [   ]

(A) 同封された、同封の   (B) 添付された、添付の   (C) 問い合わせ   (D) 返信   (E) 件名

次のメールをよく読んでみましょう。

From:	Irina Roland
To:	Jack Robinson
Subject:	Admission to the Advanced Marketing Seminar
Date:	August 15

Dear Mr. Robinson,

We are pleased to inform you that you have passed the web-test for the Advanced Marketing Seminar at the Trading Center.

The seminar will begin on October 5 and will be held every Friday of the month from 6 p.m. to 8 p.m. Top alumni will facilitate classes in *Effective Advertising* and *Analysis of Consumer Trend*. Well-known marketing researchers, Lawrence Gu and Peter Zhang will conduct *Effective Advertising* on the first and second Fridays. HK company senior vice-president, Andrew Gao will be in charge of *Analysis of Consumer Trend* on the last two Fridays of the month. The participation fee is $300. Payment includes free Internet access, marketing software and textbooks.

If you are interested in accepting this offer, please register for the seminar before September 1. For inquiries, reply to this email or call our office at 033-2859-3520.

Thank you.

Sincerely,

Irina Roland
Assistant Director

Try!

左の文書に関する以下の設問に対して、最も適切な答えを選択肢から選びましょう。 ↻CheckLink

1. What is inferred about the Advanced Marketing Seminar?

   (A) It is organized by charity members.

   (B) It has an online examination beforehand.

   (C) It is a requirement for a job application.

   (D) It is conducted by university professors.

                                          Ⓐ Ⓑ Ⓒ Ⓓ

2. Who will NOT teach one of the courses?

   (A) Lawrence Gu

   (B) Peter Zhang

   (C) Irina Roland

   (D) Andrew Gao

                                          Ⓐ Ⓑ Ⓒ Ⓓ

3. By when do the applicants need to register?

   (A) By August 15

   (B) By August 31

   (C) By October 5

   (D) By Friday

                                          Ⓐ Ⓑ Ⓒ Ⓓ

Review! **Unit 13**

☐ Part 1 における写真描写問題は、写真が撮られた「(1.   )」の
   ことを尋ねているので、選択肢に (2.   ) が使われることが多い。

☐ Part 4 の説明文では多くの場合、話に (3.   ) がある。それは、
   「(4.   )」→「(5.   )」→
   「(6.   )」という形式が多い。

☐ Part 6 では、(7.   ) が大切。空所の (8.   )
   を見るだけでなく、文全体の (9.   ) をおさえる必要がある。

☐ Part 7 では、(10.   ) 形式の文書がよく出題される。

Build Up Your TOEIC Vocabulary!

At Seminars & Workshops

単語を覚えて、30秒以内にいくつ言えるか、ペアで確認してみましょう。

手順

① 英単語を見て意味を言う役とチェックする役に分かれて、お互いの教科書を交換する。
② 英単語を見て意味を言う役は、日本語訳を筆箱などで隠す。
③ 教員の合図とともに、1～20の英単語を見て意味を言う（わからない場合は Let me skip it! と相手に伝えましょう）。
④ チェック役は相手の答えを聞き、正解していたら日本語訳の □ ボックスに左端から✓を入れる。
⑤ 同じ手順を日本語訳→英単語でも行う。

DL 161　　CD3-39

1.	lecturer	1. 講師
2.	minutes	2. 議事録
3.	vice-president	3. 副社長
4.	attendee	4. 参加者
5.	registration fee	5. 参加料、登録費用
6.	advanced	6. 上級の
7.	intermediate	7. 中級の
8.	elementary	8. 初級の
9.	admission	9. 入場
10.	reception desk	10. 受付
11.	audience	11. 聴衆
12.	venue	12. 会場
13.	accommodation	13. 宿泊施設
14.	additional	14. 追加の
15.	luncheon party	15. 昼食会
16.	handout	16. 配布資料
17.	podium	17. 演台
18.	capacity	18. 収容人数
19.	objective	19. 目的
20.	theme	20. テーマ

＊点線のところで折ると活動がしやすくなります。

TOEIC Part 1

写真描写問題

LISTENING
Check Point!

まぎらわしい発音の単語に注意しよう

Part 1 では、まぎらわしい発音の単語（walk/work、glass/grass、play/pray、ride/write など）が入った不正解の選択肢が含まれることも多くあります。しっかりとすべての選択肢を聞いた上で、様々なヒントも利用しながら正しい答えを選ぶようにしましょう。

Practice!

写真を参考にして、空所の語句を聞き取ってみましょう。

🎧 DL 162 ～ 163   💿 CD3-40 ～ 💿 CD3-41

1.

2.

1. A cameraman _____ _____ _____, shooting photos in the field.

2. Please _____ _____ _____ the headset in the center of the picture.

Try!

下の写真に関する英文が 4 つ読まれます。写真を最も適切に描写している選択肢を選びましょう。

⟳ CheckLink   🎧 DL 164 ～ 165   💿 CD3-42 ～ 💿 CD3-43

1.

Ⓐ Ⓑ Ⓒ Ⓓ

2.

Ⓐ Ⓑ Ⓒ Ⓓ

TOEIC Part **2** 応答問題

Yes / No 以外の応答表現をおさえよう

Part 2 では、質問に対する答えが常に Yes または No というわけではなく、どちらでもないような応答表現が正解となることがあります。例えば、「何時に会いますか」という質問に対して、「何時でも構いません」と答える場合などがこれにあたります。

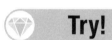

以下の応答表現の日本語訳にふさわしいものを選択肢から選びましょう。　⟲CheckLink

1. Either will be fine. 　　　　　　　　　　　　　　　　　　　[　　]
2. I haven't decided yet. 　　　　　　　　　　　　　　　　　[　　]
3. I don't mind. 　　　　　　　　　　　　　　　　　　　　[　　]
4. It depends. 　　　　　　　　　　　　　　　　　　　　　[　　]
5. I'd rather…. 　　　　　　　　　　　　　　　　　　　　[　　]

> (A) 時と場合によります　　(B) 私はむしろ…です
> (C) どちらでも結構ですよ　　(D) まだ決めていません
> (E) 構いませんよ

Try!

質問文を聞き、最も適切な答えを選択肢から選びましょう。

⟲CheckLink　🎧 DL 166 ~ 170　◎CD3-44 ~ ◎CD3-48

1. Mark your answer on your answer sheet. 　　Ⓐ　Ⓑ　Ⓒ
2. Mark your answer on your answer sheet. 　　Ⓐ　Ⓑ　Ⓒ
3. Mark your answer on your answer sheet. 　　Ⓐ　Ⓑ　Ⓒ
4. Mark your answer on your answer sheet. 　　Ⓐ　Ⓑ　Ⓒ
5. Mark your answer on your answer sheet. 　　Ⓐ　Ⓑ　Ⓒ

Improve Your TOEIC Listening Skills!

TOIEC Part 1 および Part 2 形式の音声を聞き、以下の空所を埋めましょう。1 回目は通常のスピードで、2 回目はポーズ入りの音声が流れます。その後、1 に関しては写真を最もよく描写しているものを、2 および 3 に関しては質問文に対する最も適切な答えを選択肢から選びましょう。

※各空所はすべて正解した場合に、(～～～) は 3 点、(＿＿＿) は 2 点、(＿＿＿) は 1 点として採点します（部分点はありません）。

1.

↻CheckLink 🎧 DL 171 ~ 172　◉ CD3-49　~　◉ CD3-50

(A) The women are (¹.＿＿＿＿＿＿) TV
programs.

(B) The women are standing
(².＿＿＿＿＿＿ ＿＿＿＿＿＿
＿＿＿＿＿＿) the monitors.

(C) There are some monitors
(³.＿＿＿＿＿＿ ＿＿＿＿＿＿
＿＿＿＿＿＿ ＿＿＿＿＿＿).

(D) Some monitors have been
(⁴.＿＿＿＿＿＿).　　Ⓐ Ⓑ Ⓒ Ⓓ

↻CheckLink 🎧 DL 173 ~ 174　◉ CD3-51　~　◉ CD3-52

2. (¹.＿＿＿＿＿＿ ＿＿＿＿＿＿) have you been waiting?

(A) (².＿＿＿＿＿＿ ＿＿＿＿＿＿)

(B) (³.＿＿＿＿＿＿ ＿＿＿＿＿＿ ＿＿＿＿＿＿)

(C) (⁴.＿＿＿＿＿＿ ＿＿＿＿＿＿ ＿＿＿＿＿＿), I think.　　Ⓐ Ⓑ Ⓒ

↻CheckLink 🎧 DL 175 ~ 176　◉ CD3-53　~　◉ CD3-54

3. Would you (¹.～～～～～～～) me set up the show?

(A) Yes, I met him (².＿＿＿＿＿＿ ＿＿＿＿＿＿).

(B) (³.～～～～～～～)

(C) This show is (⁴.＿＿＿＿＿＿).　　Ⓐ Ⓑ Ⓒ

Dictation Score	╱**20**

TOEIC Part **5** 短文穴埋め問題

時 制 に 強 く な ろ う

　Part 5 で出題される時制の問題では、正解へのヒントが文中に隠されている場合も多くあります。例えば、since があれば完了形、usually があれば現在形、right now があれば進行形というように、文中のヒントを活用していきましょう。

時制問題のヒントとなる語句

　現在形⇒ currently, every day (week/month), nowadays, usually

　　　過去形⇒ ago, last year (week/month), yesterday

　　　未来形⇒ in X years（X年たてば）, next month (day/week), tomorrow

　　　完了形⇒ (ever) since, for, lately, so far, until now

　　　未来完了形⇒ by＋未来の日付, in X years（X年たてば）

　　　進行形⇒ right now

Practice!

[　] 内から正しい語句を選び、文を完成させましょう。　　

1. The reporter [(A) has won / (B) wins] many prestigious prizes over the years.

2. The safe return of the missing mountain climbers [(A) is / (B) was] reported yesterday.

3. The opening date of the new research center [(A) will be / (B) is] announced tomorrow.

4. The prime minister [(A) is giving / (B) gives] a press conference right now.

Try!

空所に入る語句として最も適切な選択肢を選び、文を完成させましょう。　　

1. The governor ------- three press conferences on the corruption case so far this month.

(A) has had　　(B) had　　(C) has　　(D) is having

Ⓐ　Ⓑ　Ⓒ　Ⓓ

2. Informed sources say that the government ------- the basic planning of the new health care system by the end of this month.
(A) is finishing　　　　　(B) will have finished
(C) has been finishing　(D) has finished

Ⓐ　Ⓑ　Ⓒ　Ⓓ

3. In five years, about 20 percent of our profits ------- made by the sales of this product.
(A) would be　(B) is　(C) has been　(D) will be

Ⓐ　Ⓑ　Ⓒ　Ⓓ

4. Lately, SNS ------- a popular medium of communication among the younger generation.
(A) has become　(B) become　(C) becoming　(D) became

Ⓐ　Ⓑ　Ⓒ　Ⓓ

5. According to the newspaper, net sales of Common Market Corporation in the current year ------- 10 percent higher than those of the previous year.
(A) are　(B) had been　(C) were　(D) is

Ⓐ　Ⓑ　Ⓒ　Ⓓ

6. Some of the companies ------- market share right now because they are too slow to respond to market demands.
(A) has lost　(B) loses　(C) lost　(D) are losing

Ⓐ　Ⓑ　Ⓒ　Ⓓ

7. The movie ------- currently available on the Internet.
(A) was　(B) will be　(C) is　(D) has been

Ⓐ　Ⓑ　Ⓒ　Ⓓ

8. According to the article, in ten years or so, computers ------- taxi drivers' jobs.
(A) will replace　(B) have replaced　(C) replace　(D) are replacing

Ⓐ　Ⓑ　Ⓒ　Ⓓ

9. Ever since the massive recall of its product, financial analysts ------- difficulties for the company, according to the news broadcast.
(A) have been predicting　(B) predicts　(C) will predict　(D) predict

Ⓐ　Ⓑ　Ⓒ　Ⓓ

10. *Doraemon* ------- one of the most popular cartoon characters over the past several decades.
(A) has been　(B) have been　(C) will be　(D) is

Ⓐ　Ⓑ　Ⓒ　Ⓓ

全体か部分か、問題を見極めよう

　Part 7 の問題形式は、文書全体の内容を問うものと、特定の部分を問うものに分けることができます。全体問題に対しては、設問の冒頭（5W1H）に注意して、質問の意図をつかみましょう。部分問題に関しては、設問に含まれる疑問詞に加えて、固有名詞などに注目し、ポイントとなる情報をしぼってパッセージを読み進めるとよいでしょう。

Practice!

以下の設問は文書全体の内容を問うものなのか、部分を問うものなのか、どちらでしょう。
適切と思われるものを選択肢から選びましょう。　　　CheckLink

1. What does the notice announce? (A) 全体 (B) 部分
2. Why does Lily get the email? (A) 全体 (B) 部分
3. How frequent is the maintenance work? (A) 全体 (B) 部分
4. What is the purpose of the memo? (A) 全体 (B) 部分
5. When will Mr. Smith arrive at the office? (A) 全体 (B) 部分

次の文書をよく読んでみましょう。

Reducing Deaths from Heart Disease

　Heart disease is the world's leading cause of death. Each year over one million people suffer from heart attacks and of this number over 700,000 die. Reducing deaths from heart disease will require changes in the way people live.

　One of the main causes of heart disease is a lack of good eating habits. People should eat more fish, whole grains, vegetables, vegetable oils and nuts, and reduce the amount of salt and trans fats in their diets.

　Lack of exercise is also another risk factor. In order to keep a healthy weight, exercising at least thirty minutes on most days is effective, and it can reduce stress, too.

　There is no single cause of heart disease, but how you eat is very important. According to researchers, eating a small amount of chocolate can help people reduce the risk of heart disease. They recommend eating around 50 grams of dark chocolate each day.

Try!

左の文書に関する以下の設問に対して、最も適切な答えを選択肢から選びましょう。　⟲CheckLink

1. What is one of the main causes of heart disease?

(A) Bad eating practices

(B) Too much exercise

(C) Eating dark chocolate

(D) Lack of sleep

Ⓐ　Ⓑ　Ⓒ　Ⓓ

2. What kind of food does the report recommend?

(A) Salty food

(B) Trans fats

(C) Whole wheat

(D) Less fish

Ⓐ　Ⓑ　Ⓒ　Ⓓ

3. How much chocolate should we eat in a week to reduce the risk of heart disease?

(A) 300 grams

(B) 350 grams

(C) 400 grams

(D) 450 grams

Ⓐ　Ⓑ　Ⓒ　Ⓓ

Review!　Unit 14

☐ Part 1では、(¹.　　　　　　　　) の単語が入った不正解の選択肢が含まれることがある。

☐ Part 2 では、質問に対する答えが常に (².　　　　　　　) というわけではなく、(³.　　　　　　　) ような応答表現が正解となることがある。

☐ Part 5 の (⁴.　　　　　　　) を問う問題では、正解のヒントが (⁵.　　　　　　　) に隠されている場合も多くある。例えば、(⁶.　　　　　　) があれば完了形、(⁷.　　　　　　　) があれば現在形、(⁸.　　　　　　) があれば進行形というように、文中のヒントを活用するとよい。

☐ Part 7 の問題形式は、(⁹.　　　　　　　) の内容を問うものと、(¹⁰.　　　　　　　) を問うものに分けることができる。

Build Up Your TOEIC Vocabulary!

News & Media

単語を覚えて、30秒以内にいくつ言えるか、ペアで確認してみましょう。

手順

① 英単語を見て意味を言う役とチェックする役に分かれて、お互いの教科書を交換する。
② 英単語を見て意味を言う役は、日本語訳を筆箱などで隠す。
③ 教員の合図とともに、1〜20の英単語を見て意味を言う（わからない場合は Let me skip it! と相手に伝えましょう）。
④ チェック役は相手の答えを聞き、正解していたら日本語訳の □ ボックスに左端から✓を入れる。
⑤ 同じ手順を日本語訳→英単語でも行う。

🎧 DL 177　💿 CD3-55

1. □□□ press conference	**1.** □□□ 記者会見
2. □□□ article	**2.** □□□ 記事
3. □□□ broadcast	**3.** □□□ 放送する
4. □□□ advertisement	**4.** □□□ 広告
5. □□□ news flash	**5.** □□□ ニュース速報
6. □□□ breaking news	**6.** □□□ ニュース速報
7. □□□ reporter	**7.** □□□ 記者
8. □□□ editorial	**8.** □□□ 社説
9. □□□ opinion poll	**9.** □□□ 世論調査
10. □□□ the front page	**10.** □□□ （新聞の）一面
11. □□□ viewer	**11.** □□□ 視聴者
12. □□□ image	**12.** □□□ 画像
13. □□□ subscribe	**13.** □□□ 購読する
14. □□□ post	**14.** □□□ 投稿する
15. □□□ application (app)	**15.** □□□ アプリ
16. □□□ computer virus	**16.** □□□ コンピュータウイルス
17. □□□ portal site	**17.** □□□ ポータルサイト
18. □□□ compression	**18.** □□□ 圧縮
19. □□□ announcement	**19.** □□□ お知らせ
20. □□□ cell phone	**20.** □□□ 携帯電話

＊点線のところで折ると活動がしやすくなります。

Part 1

下の写真に関する英文が 4 つ読まれます。写真を最も適切に描写しているものを選びましょう。

⟳CheckLink ◉ CD3-56 ~ ◉ CD3-59

1.

Ⓐ Ⓑ Ⓒ Ⓓ

2.

Ⓐ Ⓑ Ⓒ Ⓓ

3.

Ⓐ Ⓑ Ⓒ Ⓓ

4.

Ⓐ Ⓑ Ⓒ Ⓓ

/4

Part 2

質問文を聞き、最も適切な答えを選択肢から選びましょう。

⟳CheckLink ◉ CD3-60 ~ ◉ CD3-66

5. Mark your answer on your answer sheet.   Ⓐ Ⓑ Ⓒ

6. Mark your answer on your answer sheet.   Ⓐ Ⓑ Ⓒ

7. Mark your answer on your answer sheet.   Ⓐ Ⓑ Ⓒ

8. Mark your answer on your answer sheet.   Ⓐ Ⓑ Ⓒ

9. Mark your answer on your answer sheet.   Ⓐ Ⓑ Ⓒ

10. Mark your answer on your answer sheet.   Ⓐ Ⓑ Ⓒ

11. Mark your answer on your answer sheet.   Ⓐ Ⓑ Ⓒ

/7

Part 3

会話を聞き、以下の設問に対して最も適切な答えを選択肢から選びましょう。

CheckLink CD3-67 ~ CD3-70

12. What are the speakers mainly talking about?

(A) The new budget reduction policy

(B) The new energy conservation policy

(C) The new employee ID card policy

(D) The new maternity leave policy

Ⓐ Ⓑ Ⓒ Ⓓ

13. When will the new card be available?

(A) On March 31　　　　　　　(B) On April 30

(C) On April 1　　　　　　　 (D) On May 1

Ⓐ Ⓑ Ⓒ Ⓓ

14. Where can the speakers get the new card?

(A) At the personnel department　(B) At the office entrance

(C) On the website　　　　　　 (D) At the café

Ⓐ Ⓑ Ⓒ Ⓓ

CheckLink CD3-71 ~ CD3-74

TIME	EVENT	ROOM
10:00 A.M.	Keynote speech	202
11:00 A.M.	Marketing workshop	204
12:00 P.M.	Lunch	208
1:00 P.M.	Panel discussion	212

15. What does the man ask the woman to do at the registration desk?

(A) Answer some questions　　 (B) Work alone for some time

(C) Register for the conference　(D) Lock up the conference room

Ⓐ Ⓑ Ⓒ Ⓓ

16. Look at the graphic. Which event will the woman take part in?

(A) Keynote speech　　　　　 (B) Marketing workshop

(C) Lunch　　　　　　　　　 (D) Panel discussion

Ⓐ Ⓑ Ⓒ Ⓓ

17. Why does John want to see the woman?

(A) To get her advice for him　 (B) To do the project together

(C) To share the marketing strategies　(D) To collect the questionnaire

Ⓐ Ⓑ Ⓒ Ⓓ

/6

Part 4

説明文を聞き、以下の設問に対して最も適切な答えを選択肢から選びましょう。

CheckLink   CD3-75 ~ CD3-78

ABORE model	
Bag 1	Boards
Bag 2	Screws
Bag 3	Bolts
Bag 4	Wrench

18. What is the speaker asking about?

(A) A refund   (B) Damaged goods

(C) Changing the goods   (D) Missing parts

Ⓐ   Ⓑ   Ⓒ   Ⓓ

19. Look at the graphic. Which bag is the speaker referring to?

(A) Bag 1   (B) Bag 2

(C) Bag 3   (D) Bag 4

Ⓐ   Ⓑ   Ⓒ   Ⓓ

20. What does the speaker say he will do this weekend?

(A) Visit his friend   (B) Host a party

(C) Travel for work   (D) Move to a new house

Ⓐ   Ⓑ   Ⓒ   Ⓓ

CheckLink   CD3-79 ~ CD3-82

21. Where most likely does the announcement take place?

(A) At a meeting   (B) At a seminar

(C) At a grocery shop   (D) At a hospital

Ⓐ   Ⓑ   Ⓒ   Ⓓ

22. When will the Q&A session be held?

(A) Before the first seminar   (B) After the first seminar

(C) After the second seminar   (D) Before the third seminar

Ⓐ   Ⓑ   Ⓒ   Ⓓ

23. What will most likely happen next?

(A) Introducing the speakers   (B) Having a discussion

(C) Going to the seminar room   (D) Reviewing some information

Ⓐ   Ⓑ   Ⓒ   Ⓓ

/6

Part 5

空所に入る語句として最も適切な選択肢を選び、文を完成させましょう。　⟳ CheckLink

24. We are planning to have a small party ------- honor of Mr. Block who had worked for the company for thirty five years.
(A) at　(B) in　(C) for　(D) on

Ⓐ　Ⓑ　Ⓒ　Ⓓ

25. New employees were informed to arrive ------- for the reception which starts at 10 a.m. at the ABC hotel.
(A) rush　(B) temporary　(C) punctually　(D) urgent

Ⓐ　Ⓑ　Ⓒ　Ⓓ

26. In an effort to attract more applicants, Lynch Internet Advertising decided to offer a ------- gym membership.
(A) complimentary　(B) competing
(C) surprisingly　(D) conversational

Ⓐ　Ⓑ　Ⓒ　Ⓓ

27. Most customers find Yellow Tail Company trustworthy ------- it provides high quality customer service for a reasonable price.
(A) due to　(B) because of　(C) since　(D) in spite of

Ⓐ　Ⓑ　Ⓒ　Ⓓ

28. We have some good information ------- to satisfy your needs.
(A) dependable　(B) available　(C) recommend　(D) provide

Ⓐ　Ⓑ　Ⓒ　Ⓓ

29. I wouldn't have started the new project if I ------- the article by chance.
(A) don't read　(B) didn't read　(C) hadn't read　(D) am not reading

Ⓐ　Ⓑ　Ⓒ　Ⓓ

30. Do not forget ------- the changes in the wordings of the final agreement.
(A) checking　(B) have checked　(C) to check　(D) check

Ⓐ　Ⓑ　Ⓒ　Ⓓ

31. Only ------- knowledge is required to operate the new system.
(A) a few　(B) a little　(C) hardly　(D) few

Ⓐ　Ⓑ　Ⓒ　Ⓓ

32. Chinese cuisine in the U.S. is three times ------- expensive as that in China.
(A) much　(B) more　(C) than　(D) as

Ⓐ　Ⓑ　Ⓒ　Ⓓ

33. We have gotten accustomed ------- the rules set by the new boss.
(A) to observe　(B) observe　(C) to observing　(D) have observed

Ⓐ　Ⓑ　Ⓒ　Ⓓ

34. We are planning to hire someone ------- first language is Chinese.

(A) who　　(B) which　　(C) whom　　(D) whose

Ⓐ Ⓑ Ⓒ Ⓓ

35. The meeting was ------- scheduled at 10:30 a.m. today, but it was cancelled due to the typhoon.

(A) original　　(B) originality　　(C) originally　　(D) originate

Ⓐ Ⓑ Ⓒ Ⓓ

36. This is the first time that I have ------- the Annual NY Exhibition for Mobile Phones and Devices.

(A) attended　　(B) to attended　　(C) attending　　(D) to attending

Ⓐ Ⓑ Ⓒ Ⓓ

/13

Part 6

次の文を読み、空所に入る語句として最も適切な選択肢を選びましょう。　　⟳CheckLink

Social Media: A World of Possibilities

Ten years ago, marketing options for small business owners were fairly -------.
37.
Traditional media like radio, TV and even most print advertising were just too expensive for small businesses.

-------. Email marketing, social media, blogs, and pay per click advertising offer
38.
small business owners the chance to get their messages across. -------, you could
39.
create the illusion that your company was much ------- with the help of a great
40.
website and a strong social media program.

---

37. (A) limitation　　(B) limited　　(C) limiting　　(D) limit

Ⓐ Ⓑ Ⓒ Ⓓ

38. (A) Also, marketing researchers published a report.

(B) Then, it caught the attention of social media.

(C) But print advertising should not be underestimated.

(D) Then, along came the Internet.

Ⓐ Ⓑ Ⓒ Ⓓ

39. (A) Personally　　(B) Incidentally　　(C) Essentially　　(D) Suddenly

Ⓐ Ⓑ Ⓒ Ⓓ

40. (A) large　　(B) larger　　(C) the largest　　(D) less large

Ⓐ Ⓑ Ⓒ Ⓓ

/4

Part 7

次の文書を読み、設問に対して最も適切な答えを選択肢から選びましょう。

Vessel's High Speed Internet Service
Enjoy our fast Internet speeds to suit every need

With our advanced digital network, Vessel's High Speed Internet, established last year, provides the reliability that keeps you connected to everything you want. You can video chat with friends and family, work from the home office or just watch a movie, with complete confidence.

Standard Plan $30 / month	Premium Plan $60 / month
· Get speeds up to 100Mbps. · Shop online and download music. · Includes nationwide Wi-Fi hotspot access.	· Get speeds up to 1Gbps. · Shop online and download music. · Includes nationwide and worldwide Wi-Fi hotspot access.

---

41. What can be inferred about the company from the text?

(A) It is open seven days a week.

(B) It is a relatively new company.

(C) It is operated by a large telecommunications company.

(D) It centers on Wi-Fi hotspot access service.

Ⓐ Ⓑ Ⓒ Ⓓ

42. What service is available only on the Premium Plan?

(A) Music downloading

(B) Online shopping

(C) Nationwide Wi-Fi

(D) Worldwide Wi-Fi

Ⓐ Ⓑ Ⓒ Ⓓ

次の文書を読み、設問に対して最も適切な答えを選択肢から選びましょう。　

> Alice Park, 9:28 A.M.
> I've got a call from a client. She's interested in the property for sale in the downtown area. Would it be possible to arrange a tour?

> Ray Ellis, 9:29 A.M.
> I think so. Is it the office building across Walter Street from the bank?

> Alice Park, 9:30 A.M.
> Yes, that's the one. For more information about the property, you'll need to speak with the real estate agent in charge of our commercial properties in the downtown area.

> Ray Ellis, 9:33 A.M.
> OK. Can I have the phone number, then?

> Alice Park, 9:34 A.M.
> Sorry, I don't have it. I'm sure Kevin knows, though.

43. What is probably true about the property?
- (A) It is near the bank.
- (B) It is popular.
- (C) It is cheap.
- (D) Walter owns the property.

Ⓐ　Ⓑ　Ⓒ　Ⓓ

44. Why does Mr. Ellis need to speak with the real estate agent?
- (A) To confirm the price
- (B) To check the place
- (C) To get more information
- (D) To negotiate with the client

Ⓐ　Ⓑ　Ⓒ　Ⓓ

45. At 9:34 A.M., what does Ms. Park most likely mean when she writes, "I'm sure Kevin knows, though"?
- (A) Kevin used to work for the real estate agent.
- (B) She suggests that Mr. Ellis contact Kevin.
- (C) She suggests that Kevin knows how to arrange a tour.
- (D) Kevin is going to give the information about the property.

Ⓐ　Ⓑ　Ⓒ　Ⓓ

WAREHOUSES for Lease

	Rent (per month)	Constructed in	Space (square feet)	Height	Location
Warehouse #1	$3,499	2007	10,000 SF	12-foot ceiling	Brooklyn
	Note: Shared by multiple businesses				
Warehouse #2	$5,500	2017	12,000 SF	11 to 26-foot ceiling	Brooklyn
	Note: Desired term length is 5 years.				
Warehouse #3	$4,500	2010	20,000 SF	15-foot ceiling	A few miles outside of Brooklyn
	Note: Equipped with a temperature-controlled storage				

*All locations have a state-of-the-art security system.
Please contact us by email using the contact form.

▌Contact Us
Please fill this form.

Henry Woo

h.woo@befresh.com

Your Phone Number (optional)

Your Web Site (optional)

Type your message here…

My name is Henry Woo, and I work for fruit import & export company, Befresh. I am currently looking for a warehouse in the Brooklyn area. I saw your warehouse list and I'd like to ask you their availability. I think the best option for our business will be Warehouse #3. Since our company deals with fresh products, we prefer a temperature-controlled storage. If possible, I'd like to take a tour of Warehouse #3.

Please contact me by email.

To:	Henry Woo < h.woo@befresh.com>
From:	Kris Alan <krisalan@tumberelewarehouse.com>
Subject:	A warehouse
Date:	March 4

Dear Mr. Woo,

Thank you for your inquiry. I'm Kris Alan, a customer manager of Tumberele Warehouse. As it is mentioned in the advertisement, Warehouse #3 has cool room storage (-10 to +5 Celsius). However, it is currently under negotiation. They will give us a final decision by this weekend, so I will let you know as soon as we figure it out.

Also, our new warehouse near the Brooklyn area will open next month. It has a 16,200 square feet warehouse space and 23-foot ceiling height. In addition, we can offer cool room storage or cold room storage (-25 to 0 Celsius) with this warehouse. I couldn't find the information regarding its rental fee. However, I think it would be around 4,500 to 5,000 dollars per month. Of course, that warehouse also has a state-of-the-art security system. If you are interested, please let me know.

All the best,

Kris Alan

Customer Manager, Tumberele Warehouse

46. What is the purpose of the advertisement?
(A) To rent out an industrial space
(B) To show the construction sites
(C) To ensure the arrival of a shipment
(D) To advertise a property sale

Ⓐ Ⓑ Ⓒ Ⓓ

47. Who most likely is Mr. Woo?
(A) A warehouse manager
(B) A truck driver
(C) A security guard
(D) A company employee

Ⓐ Ⓑ Ⓒ Ⓓ

48. According to Mr. Woo, what option does the company need for the warehouse?

(A) A spacious space

(B) A cooling system

(C) Easy access to the airport

(D) Parking lots

Ⓐ   Ⓑ   Ⓒ   Ⓓ

49. According to the e-mail, what information is NOT certain?

(A) Price

(B) Location

(C) Security

(D) Size

Ⓐ   Ⓑ   Ⓒ   Ⓓ

50. In the e-mail, the word "state-of-the-art" in paragraph 2, line 5, is closest in meaning to

(A) cutting-edge

(B) artistic

(C) informative

(D) descriptive

Ⓐ   Ⓑ   Ⓒ   Ⓓ

∕10

Total   ∕50

Review Test 1 解答用紙

学籍番号
ふりがな
名 前

LISTENING SECTION

Part 1

No.	ANSWER			
	A	B	C	D
1	Ⓐ	Ⓑ	Ⓒ	Ⓓ
2	Ⓐ	Ⓑ	Ⓒ	Ⓓ
3	Ⓐ	Ⓑ	Ⓒ	Ⓓ
4	Ⓐ	Ⓑ	Ⓒ	Ⓓ

Part 2

No.	ANSWER			
	A	B	C	
5	Ⓐ	Ⓑ	Ⓒ	
6	Ⓐ	Ⓑ	Ⓒ	
7	Ⓐ	Ⓑ	Ⓒ	
8	Ⓐ	Ⓑ	Ⓒ	

No.	ANSWER			
	A	B	C	
9	Ⓐ	Ⓑ	Ⓒ	
10	Ⓐ	Ⓑ	Ⓒ	
11	Ⓐ	Ⓑ	Ⓒ	

Part 3

No.	ANSWER			
	A	B	C	D
12	Ⓐ	Ⓑ	Ⓒ	Ⓓ
13	Ⓐ	Ⓑ	Ⓒ	Ⓓ
14	Ⓐ	Ⓑ	Ⓒ	Ⓓ

No.	ANSWER			
	A	B	C	D
15	Ⓐ	Ⓑ	Ⓒ	Ⓓ
16	Ⓐ	Ⓑ	Ⓒ	Ⓓ
17	Ⓐ	Ⓑ	Ⓒ	Ⓓ

Part 4

No.	ANSWER			
	A	B	C	D
18	Ⓐ	Ⓑ	Ⓒ	Ⓓ
19	Ⓐ	Ⓑ	Ⓒ	Ⓓ
20	Ⓐ	Ⓑ	Ⓒ	Ⓓ

No.	ANSWER			
	A	B	C	D
21	Ⓐ	Ⓑ	Ⓒ	Ⓓ
22	Ⓐ	Ⓑ	Ⓒ	Ⓓ
23	Ⓐ	Ⓑ	Ⓒ	Ⓓ

READING SECTION

Part 5

No.	ANSWER			
	A	B	C	D
24	Ⓐ	Ⓑ	Ⓒ	Ⓓ
25	Ⓐ	Ⓑ	Ⓒ	Ⓓ
26	Ⓐ	Ⓑ	Ⓒ	Ⓓ
27	Ⓐ	Ⓑ	Ⓒ	Ⓓ
28	Ⓐ	Ⓑ	Ⓒ	Ⓓ

No.	ANSWER			
	A	B	C	D
29	Ⓐ	Ⓑ	Ⓒ	Ⓓ
30	Ⓐ	Ⓑ	Ⓒ	Ⓓ
31	Ⓐ	Ⓑ	Ⓒ	Ⓓ
32	Ⓐ	Ⓑ	Ⓒ	Ⓓ
33	Ⓐ	Ⓑ	Ⓒ	Ⓓ

Part 6

No.	ANSWER			
	A	B	C	D
34	Ⓐ	Ⓑ	Ⓒ	Ⓓ
35	Ⓐ	Ⓑ	Ⓒ	Ⓓ
36	Ⓐ	Ⓑ	Ⓒ	Ⓓ

No.	ANSWER			
	A	B	C	D
37	Ⓐ	Ⓑ	Ⓒ	Ⓓ
38	Ⓐ	Ⓑ	Ⓒ	Ⓓ
39	Ⓐ	Ⓑ	Ⓒ	Ⓓ
40	Ⓐ	Ⓑ	Ⓒ	Ⓓ

Part 7

No.	ANSWER			
	A	B	C	D
41	Ⓐ	Ⓑ	Ⓒ	Ⓓ
42	Ⓐ	Ⓑ	Ⓒ	Ⓓ
43	Ⓐ	Ⓑ	Ⓒ	Ⓓ
44	Ⓐ	Ⓑ	Ⓒ	Ⓓ
45	Ⓐ	Ⓑ	Ⓒ	Ⓓ

No.	ANSWER			
	A	B	C	D
46	Ⓐ	Ⓑ	Ⓒ	Ⓓ
47	Ⓐ	Ⓑ	Ⓒ	Ⓓ
48	Ⓐ	Ⓑ	Ⓒ	Ⓓ
49	Ⓐ	Ⓑ	Ⓒ	Ⓓ
50	Ⓐ	Ⓑ	Ⓒ	Ⓓ

Review Test 2 解答用紙

学籍番号

ふりがな

名　前

LISTENING SECTION

Part 1

No.	ANSWER A B C D
1	Ⓐ Ⓑ Ⓒ Ⓓ
2	Ⓐ Ⓑ Ⓒ Ⓓ
3	Ⓐ Ⓑ Ⓒ Ⓓ
4	Ⓐ Ⓑ Ⓒ Ⓓ

Part 2

No.	ANSWER A B C
5	Ⓐ Ⓑ Ⓒ
6	Ⓐ Ⓑ Ⓒ
7	Ⓐ Ⓑ Ⓒ
8	Ⓐ Ⓑ Ⓒ
9	Ⓐ Ⓑ Ⓒ
10	Ⓐ Ⓑ Ⓒ
11	Ⓐ Ⓑ Ⓒ

Part 3

No.	ANSWER A B C D
12	Ⓐ Ⓑ Ⓒ Ⓓ
13	Ⓐ Ⓑ Ⓒ Ⓓ
14	Ⓐ Ⓑ Ⓒ Ⓓ
15	Ⓐ Ⓑ Ⓒ Ⓓ
16	Ⓐ Ⓑ Ⓒ Ⓓ
17	Ⓐ Ⓑ Ⓒ Ⓓ

Part 4

No.	ANSWER A B C D
18	Ⓐ Ⓑ Ⓒ Ⓓ
19	Ⓐ Ⓑ Ⓒ Ⓓ
20	Ⓐ Ⓑ Ⓒ Ⓓ
21	Ⓐ Ⓑ Ⓒ Ⓓ
22	Ⓐ Ⓑ Ⓒ Ⓓ
23	Ⓐ Ⓑ Ⓒ Ⓓ

READING SECTION

Part 5

No.	ANSWER A B C D
24	Ⓐ Ⓑ Ⓒ Ⓓ
25	Ⓐ Ⓑ Ⓒ Ⓓ
26	Ⓐ Ⓑ Ⓒ Ⓓ
27	Ⓐ Ⓑ Ⓒ Ⓓ
28	Ⓐ Ⓑ Ⓒ Ⓓ
29	Ⓐ Ⓑ Ⓒ Ⓓ
30	Ⓐ Ⓑ Ⓒ Ⓓ
31	Ⓐ Ⓑ Ⓒ Ⓓ
32	Ⓐ Ⓑ Ⓒ Ⓓ
33	Ⓐ Ⓑ Ⓒ Ⓓ

Part 6

No.	ANSWER A B C D
34	Ⓐ Ⓑ Ⓒ Ⓓ
35	Ⓐ Ⓑ Ⓒ Ⓓ
36	Ⓐ Ⓑ Ⓒ Ⓓ
37	Ⓐ Ⓑ Ⓒ Ⓓ
38	Ⓐ Ⓑ Ⓒ Ⓓ
39	Ⓐ Ⓑ Ⓒ Ⓓ
40	Ⓐ Ⓑ Ⓒ Ⓓ

Part 7

No.	ANSWER A B C D
41	Ⓐ Ⓑ Ⓒ Ⓓ
42	Ⓐ Ⓑ Ⓒ Ⓓ
43	Ⓐ Ⓑ Ⓒ Ⓓ
44	Ⓐ Ⓑ Ⓒ Ⓓ
45	Ⓐ Ⓑ Ⓒ Ⓓ
46	Ⓐ Ⓑ Ⓒ Ⓓ
47	Ⓐ Ⓑ Ⓒ Ⓓ
48	Ⓐ Ⓑ Ⓒ Ⓓ
49	Ⓐ Ⓑ Ⓒ Ⓓ
50	Ⓐ Ⓑ Ⓒ Ⓓ

MEMO

MEMO

本書には CD（別売）があります

ILLUMINATING THE PATH TO THE
TOEIC® L&R TEST

新・重点特化型 TOEIC®L&Rテスト実力養成

2021年1月20日　初版第1刷発行
2024年2月20日　初版第5刷発行

著　者　　植 木 美 千 子
　　　　　Brent Cotsworth
　　　　　山 岡 浩 一
　　　　　竹 内 　 理

発行者　　福 岡 正 人
発行所　　株式会社　**金 星 堂**

（〒101-0051）東京都千代田区神田神保町3-21
Tel. (03) 3263-3828（営業部）
　　 (03) 3263-3997（編集部）
Fax (03) 3263-0716
https://www.kinsei-do.co.jp

編集担当　今門貴浩　　　　　　　　　　Printed in Japan
印刷所・製本所／萩原印刷株式会社

ISBN978-4-7647-4127-0　C1082